ANYONE CA

Welcome to the most comprehensive examination of the history and practical use of scrying ever presented. Donald Tyson, a hereditary seer and ceremonial magician, has used the scrying techniques presented within this book with great success in his own magical work.

Tyson guides you through a variety of scrying techniques so you can begin to scry with confidence. Try crystal gazing, pendulums, black mirrors, Ouija™ boards, dowsing rods, aura reading, psychometry, automatic writing, channeling, and more. Also, be one of the few to experience the coveted ancient techniques of Babylonian oil scrying, fire gazing, Egyptian lamp scrying, water scrying, wind scrying, ink scrying, shell-hearing, and oracular dreaming.

If you have latent psychic ability and want to develop it, or simply wish to learn more about the history and many techniques of scrying, you will find the necessary information and tools you need in *Scrying for Beginners*.

ABOUT THE AUTHOR

Donald Tyson is a Canadian from Halifax, Nova Scotia. Early in life he was drawn to science by an intense fascination with astronomy, building a telescope by hand when he was eight. He began university seeking a science degree, but became disillusioned with the aridity and futility of a mechanistic view of the universe and shifted his major to English. After graduating with honors he has pursued a writing career.

Now he devotes his life to the attainment of a complete gnosis of the art of magic in theory and practice. His purpose is to formulate an accessible system of personal training composed of East and West, past and present, that will help the individual discover the reason for one's existence and a way to fulfill it.

TO WRITE TO THE AUTHOR

If you would like to contact the author or would like more information about this book, please write to him in care of Llewellyn Worldwide. We cannot guarantee every letter will be answered, but all will be forwarded. Please write to:

Donald Tyson
℅ Llewellyn Worldwide
2143 Wooddale Drive
Woodbury, MN 55125-2989

Please enclose a self-addressed, stamped envelope for reply or $1.00 to cover costs.

If outside the U.S.A., enclose international postal reply coupon.

SCRYING
for BEGINNERS

Tapping into the Supersensory Powers of Your Subconscious

Donald Tyson

Llewellyn Publications
Woodbury, Minnesota

FIRST EDITION
Twelfth Printing, 2013

Cover design: Adrienne Zimiga
Cover Image: © Mixa/SuperStock
Book design: Laura Gudbaur
Project Coordinator: Darwin Holmstrom
Layout: Virginia Sutton

Library of Congress Cataloging-in-Publication Data
Tyson, Donald, 1954-
Scrying for beginners: tapping into the supersensory powers of your subconscious / Donald Tyson—1st ed.
    p.   cm.
Includes bibliographical references (p.   )
ISBN 13: 978-1-56718-746-5
ISBN 10: 1-56718-746-3 (pbk.)
1.Automatism. 2.Crystal gazing. I. Title. II. Series.
BF1321.T87   1997
133.3--dc21   96-50071
                                                         CIP

Llewellyn Publications
A Division of Llewellyn Worldwide Ltd.
2143 Wooddale Drive
Woodbury, Minnesota 55125-2989
Llewellyn is a registered trademark of Llewellyn Worldwide Ltd.

Printed in the United States of America

OTHER TITLES BY DONALD TYSON

Ritual Magic
The Messenger (fiction)
Power of the Word (formerly titled *Tetragrammaton*)
Enochian Magic for Beginners
Familiar Spirits
1-2-3 Tarot
Necronomicon (fiction)
Soul Flight
Alhazred (fiction)
Portable Magic
The 13 Gates of the Necronomicon
The Fourth Book of Occult Philosophy
Grimoire of the Necronomicon
Runic Astrology
Demonology of King James I

EDITOR AND ANNOTATOR

Three Books of Occult Philosophy
  Written by Henry Cornelius Agrippa of
  Nettesheim

CARDS AND KITS

Necronomicon Tarot Kit

Contents

Tales of My Grandfather

"THE STRONGEST LITTLE MAN IN CAPE BRETON"

When I was a young boy I remember listening for hours on end to my mother as she related stories of her father, my grandfather. In his youth in Yorkshire, England, he had worked as a circus acrobat and strongman before marrying my grandmother and emigrating to Nova Scotia to mine coal. He continued to lift enormous weights with his teeth, walk the tightrope, perform trick ice-skating feats, ride a unicycle, and practice his other circus skills in his new homeland.

A body builder of the Charles Atlas school before such things were fashionable, he taught boxing and wrestling to supplement his mining income, which came from loading coal into steel carts for transport to the surface. A flat fee was paid for each box loaded. My grandfather always loaded more on his shift than any other miner. He was known far and wide as the "strongest little man in Cape Breton," and regularly challenged body builders, who came to Nova Scotia teaching courses in physical culture, to a public competition of muscle display at the local theater. Most declined.

He was also a scryer. Where he learned this occult trade is uncertain. He may have picked it up during his wild, early days under the big top. Or he may have gained it through his association with a spiritualist church in Chicago led by a preacher named Mrs. Lord. I know nothing about this woman, but as a child her name struck me as singularly appropriate for someone who talked to spirits.

He had always read cards (regular playing cards — Tarot decks were scarce in those days), palms, and tea leaves for anyone who came to the house seeking his advice about personal matters. For these services he never charged a penny, but those who visited were told that they could leave a gift of whatever they felt was appropriate. Apparently there was no shortage of neighbors seeking to benefit from his psychic skills. He was as famous for his readings as for his strong-man stunts.

MY GRANDFATHER'S CRYSTAL

One day he sent twenty-five dollars through the mail for a crystal ball (more than a week's wages in the early 1920s). It came from the United States, probably from the de Laurence Company in Chicago — there were no crystal balls to be had in Nova Scotia. This globe presently resides with one of my uncles. It is an unremarkable article to look at, about four inches in diameter and made out of a cloudy glass flawed with small bubbles. Nonetheless, he was able to achieve results with it that are legendary, at least within my family, and if true are little short of miraculous.

Once he predicted for a client the death of a sister living in England. The client had received a letter that same day but had not yet been home to open it, having gone home with my grandfather immediately after leaving work at the coal pit. When he opened the letter he discovered that it contained news of his sister's death. My mother had numerous other wondrous tales to relate, most of which I have unfortunately forgotten.

GRANDFATHER'S METHOD

The method of my grandfather was quite simple. He constructed a small box out of wood about the size of a square shoe box and lined the inside with black velvet. This box had a hinged door that opened on the top. Within it he kept his crystal ball on its small wooden stand. When he wished to gaze into the crystal, he would set the box on the kitchen table and open the lid, then completely cover the box and his head and shoulders with a large piece of black velvet as he sat on a chair before the table peering through the darkness at the crystal.

This always struck my mother as very odd, because, as she said, it would have been impossible to see the crystal itself, never mind what was inside the crystal, so she and the rest of the family always wondered what he was staring at. My grandfather was uncharacteristically close-mouthed about his crystal visions. He would not talk about them. When anybody asked him about the crystal, he put them off and began to talk about something else.

MY PSYCHIC INHERITANCE

Whether there is any truth in the claim that second sight is an inherited gift is open to debate. However, my mother claimed to scry visions at night just before going to sleep. They came to her, she said, in the form of tiny, distant images, similar to pictures viewed through the wrong end of a telescope. She never tried to develop this talent in any way. It frightened her.

Perhaps some small portion of my grandfather's gift has descended to me. At the very least, it caused me to have a lifelong fascination with the occult and paranormal. This eventually resulted in my systematic study of magic in all its forms, and in the book that you are presently reading.

As was true of my grandfather, I do not believe it is proper for me to discuss in detail my own personal experiences as a scryer. Some matters are too private and too hallowed to put on public display. I will say only that I do have some ability as a scryer, though I am not nearly as accomplished as my grandfather.

Too many basic introductions to scrying and other psychic phenomena are written by journalists or professional freelancers who gather up a few newspaper clippings, spend a couple of afternoons doing research in the local library, then throw their material together into a smoothly written but shallow book of hearsay and history. These hack authors have no firsthand knowledge of scrying. Nothing that they write is based on their personal experience.

You, the reader, have the right to know that this book was written by someone who scries. I have experimented with most of the techniques described in the following chapters, including water divination, the crystal, the pendulum, the black mirror, the Ouija board, fire scrying, smoke scrying, wind scrying, and dream scrying. I am also skilled at numerous forms of divination by lots such as geomancy, the Tarot, the runes, and the I Ching. From time to time I have communicated successfully with spirits.

PURPOSE OF THIS BOOK

This book was written with the hope that I can pass on some of the enthusiasm I feel in my own heart every time I sit down before the mirror or the crystal and seek to lift the rolling gray clouds that obscure their depths. It is for beginners who think they may also have inherited some talent for seership from their ancestors, but do not know how to develop their skills or practice their chosen art.

My purpose has been to present as broad an overview as possible of all the many instruments of scrying that have proven practical and effective down through the centuries since the days of the ancient Egyptians. I have also attempted to link these numerous divergent techniques with a simple definition of the general psychological mechanism of scrying.

It may not seem at first glance that crystal gazing, the Ouija board, and dowsing are all expressions of the same occult art, but this is indeed the case. As I will demonstrate in the following chapters, scrying cannot be defined by the instruments it employs, or even by the physical senses that act as the avenues for these instruments. Scrying is a psychological technique to deliberately acquire information by extrasensory means through the unconscious mind, which then makes it intelligible to the conscious mind in the form of what I call sensory metaphors.

Sensory metaphors are packets of information shaped by the unconscious mind into patterns we seem to perceive with our physical senses. They include images, sounds, tactile sensations, smells, and tastes, but also such things as a vague feeling of dread or overpowering sorrow, and the involuntary physical movements that direct such tools of divination as the Ouija board, the pendulum, and the dowsing rod. Involuntary muscle contractions such as those that turn down a dowsing rod when it is held over a water source are merely another form of sensory metaphor.

WHAT THIS BOOK CONTAINS

Scrying in its narrow sense might be defined as an occult method for obtaining oracular visions in water, glass, or crystal. This is how the term is usually understood. Certainly, sight is the most vital and informative of the human senses. For this reason special emphasis is placed on visual scrying techniques, which have such a long and honorable history.

Two of the most famous of all scryers, the French astrologer Nostradamus and the English magician Dr. John Dee, have been examined in detail. I have provided a complete reconstruction of their scrying techniques, based on historical research and my own personal experience as a magician and scryer. The methods of Nostradamus and Dee are sure to fascinate all those who seek to acquire this venerable art.

I have also included a number of ancient scrying methods that are not to be easily found elsewhere, among them the Babylonian oil method and the Egyptian dream oracle method. They arise out of the same general psychological principles that govern all forms of scrying, and are quite workable even after the passage of three thousand years.

In order to make the various forms of scrying available to you in a practical way, I have given a simple ritual framework within which you may conduct most of the techniques. This serves both to make the scryings more effective and to protect the scryer from undesirable side effects. Two sets of mental exercises, simple and advanced, are set forth in detail. With regular practice they will open your conscious mind to the messages sent from your unconscious, and remove the blocks that may in the past have prevented you from achieving success with such tools as the crystal ball or the Ouija board.

Part One contains a comprehensive definition of scrying, examines who makes the best scryers, and gives the visualization exercises designed to awaken your latent talent as a seer. It provides the necessary theoretical background for a balanced understanding of this art and prepares you to actually begin to scry. Part Two contains a wide array of scrying systems employed in Western culture that have proven effective down through the centuries. Some, such as the Ouija board, have modern forms but are based on ancient methods. I have attempted to trace the history of each system back to its origins, and have given instructions about how to effectively use it today.

It is hoped that you will find in these pages everything you may have wished to know about this fascinating and romantic subject, and through the practical techniques and exercises given will quickly and with a minimum of effort be able to open the third eye of second sight upon the undiscovered country of the future, and beyond.

PART I

Preliminaries

Part I

Preliminaries

CHAPTER 1

What Is Scrying?

DEFINITION OF SCRYING

Scrying is the deliberate act of perceiving events that lie beyond the range of the physical senses by using the agents of the unconscious mind.

The scryer is separated from the things scried by distance, by time, or by levels of consciousness. Usually visual images are scried, but it is possible to scry sounds, scents, sensations, and flavors. Any impression you can pick up with the senses of your body can also be received at a distance by your mind alone through scrying.

When you watch a television program you are not scrying because the image on the screen is actually there directly in front of you, even though it may have been filmed months or years ago in a distant country. The same is true when you listen to the radio or use the telephone. The sound comes out of the speaker and goes into your physical ear, even though the original source of the sound is many miles away.

Neither are you scrying during your ordinary dreams. The images in a common dream come unsought, and the dreamer has no conscious intention to observe them. Similarly, an unconscious seer or prophet is not a scryer because the visions received by a prophet are sent without warning, and the prophet has no control over them. Clairvoyance, because it is automatic and comes unsought, is a form of prophetic vision, not a type of scrying.

On the other hand, psychometry, which seeks to perceive by touch details about a person or place from some object that has been in contact with that person or place, is a form of scrying because it is a deliberate technique of perception at a distance that transcends the limitations of the ordinary senses.

Telepathy is a form of scrying when it is consciously used to read the thoughts or emotions of another human being, because this information is not available through the senses. It exists on a level of awareness separate from the consciousness of the scryer. The scryer is able to bridge the distance between his or her own mind and the mind of the subject by a deliberate act of will.

Dowsing is a type of scrying, because the movements of the dowsing rod are messages sent from the deep mind through the nerves and muscles of the body to the consciousness. The same is true of the Ouija board, the pendulum, automatic writing, and automatic speaking.

Divination is not scrying. In divination we interpret the occult meaning of physical objects or events observed by our physical senses according to a set of established rules. It is not necessary during divination to receive data from our unconscious mind, although this sometimes happens. When it does, the divination becomes a scrying. Palm reading and Tarot reading are examples of divination.

How Scrying Works

The word "scry" literally means to see. Most forms of scrying involve the use of sight. It is important to understand that the images seen during scrying are not transmitted through the eyes. They are like the images we see in dreams. Even though they appear to be right in front of us, and we seem to be looking at them through our eyes, when we wake up we realize this was only an illusion. Our eyes were closed and the room in which we slept was dark. We could not have seen anything.

In scrying we see only with the mind. But the mind needs some way to convey the information to our conscious awareness. It must take the information we gain during a scrying session and translate that information into terms we can understand. It does this by turning the scried data into a sense impression.

Usually the mind translates the information into a still image or moving vision. Sometimes it translates it into sounds or voices. Both these forms of sense impression are very valuable because they are able to convey a large amount of specific meaning that is easy to interpret. Sometimes during scrying the mind translates its data into tactile sensations or odors. On rare occasions it even conveys information in the form of a taste in the mouth. These types of sensory impressions are not nearly as useful as sight and hearing because the data they convey is much more difficult to interpret. How do we know what the scent of violets means, or the touch of a hand upon our cheek?

Sometimes the information picked up by the deep mind during scrying cannot be accurately translated into sensory forms. When this happens the mind conveys it to our consciousness the best way it can. We may suddenly feel a sense of danger, or become afraid for no reason, or burst out laughing, or grow dizzy. This sort of experience during scrying indicates that the deep mind is struggling to communicate some bit of information that cannot be translated into impressions of sight, sound, touch, smell, or taste.

In dowsing the unconscious conveys the information we seek—the presence of water, or oil, or some mineral beneath the surface of the ground—by causing the muscles of our hands to relax and allow the dowsing wand, which is held under tension, to rotate over the correct spot. This is the mind's way of saying "dig here." Similarly, when we seek information through the Ouija board, our unconscious mind communicates it to us by controlling the movement of our hands and arms so that the planchette spells out meaningful words. Dowsing and the use of the Ouija board may not seem like forms of scrying, but the psychological mechanism is essentially the same.

AUTOMATISM

Psychologists have given a technical name to this mechanism. They call it automatism, and define it as functions or inhibitions of the body not controlled by the conscious self. There are two types of automatism. Motor automatism, sometimes called active automatism, concerns movements of the body beyond the conscious will. Sensory automatism, sometimes called passive automatism, concerns stimulation of the senses by the unconscious mind. Both classes are at root the same, and involve the transmission of a message from the unconscious mind to the conscious mind.

As you can see, the definition of automatism used by psychologists is much broader than the personal definition I have given for scrying. Automatism includes experiences that are not sought by the conscious will, such as ordinary dreams, sleep-walking, and spontaneous prophetic visions. Even so, it can provide a useful way of dividing the various types of scrying that we will examine in the coming chapters. Below I have listed the major types of scrying treated in this book under the two branches of automatism.

Sensory Automatism	**Motor Automatism**
Crystal gazing	Ouija board
Oil scrying	Dowsing rod
Ink scrying	Pendulum
Mirror gazing	Automatic writing
Fire watching	Automatic drawing
Lamp scrying	Automatic speaking
Aura reading	
Psychometry	
Shell hearing	
Dream scrying	

SENSORY METAPHORS

We can better understand the process of scrying if we consider how a computer works. All of the information entered into a computer by its programmers is in the form of binary code. This consists of strings of 1s and 0s, which really just tell the computer when to turn its millions of silicon switches on or off. If the computer were to put this information on its screen in an intermediary rather than a final form, it would be meaningless to the average person. Yet the computer is able to turn this string of binary coding into words, numbers, colors, graphics, photographs, motion pictures, and music. The computer translates its raw data into sensory impressions that human beings are able to understand.

The unconscious mind is, among other things, an extraordinarily powerful computer. It processes millions of bits of data every second, changing the raw electrical impulses from our physical senses into useful information that we need to perform the ordinary tasks of our everyday lives.

When we begin to scry, we send a message to our unconscious that we are seeking information that is beyond the reach of our senses. The unconscious mind is able to access this information, but it faces a dilemma. How can it pass along this information to our conscious awareness in a form that we are able to understand? Our consciousness is entirely made up of sensory impressions. We are aware only of things we can see, hear, feel, smell, or touch, either directly through our physical senses, or through dreams or memories.

Our unconscious mind solves this problem by shaping the information it has obtained for us in extrasensory ways into sensory metaphors. This works fine when the information concerns a real person or place—we "see" that person or place as though we where physically present. However, when the information scried is more complicated, or consists of nonphysical beings and localities, the mind has a more difficult time translating it into images or sounds that we can understand. The result is that often what we see when scrying is distorted or only an approximation of the real events we seek to perceive. It must be interpreted and analyzed before it can be used.

This has led many critics to dismiss scrying as unreliable. True, it will never be as useful as the video camera or the telephone for transmitting factual information about the physical world over a distance. However, events can be scried that cannot be recorded on machines. It is possible to scry hidden objects, or lost persons. Locked chambers and sealed vessels, or places beneath the sea or deep under the earth or remote in space can be scried, even when they are out of reach of microphones and cameras. Scrying can extend awareness across the gulf of time into the distant past or the far future. Most wonderful of all, the scryer can explore the secret realms of the mind and peer into nonphysical realities where spirits dwell.

PSYCHEDELIC EXPERIENCE

During the 1960s many persons were astonished by the sensory distortions that occurred when they took LSD. Small things grew very large, and large things seemed tiny. Human faces appeared to melt and run like wax. Time moved at a glacial pace or rushed along like an out-of-control locomotive. Acid trippers were able to "hear" colors and to "see" sounds. Sometimes they reported seeing beautiful colors that do not exist in everyday human consciousness.

LSD short-circuits the normal sensory processing function of the unconscious mind. This is why trippers are able to "see" music and "hear" colors. It also allows data that the mind would not normally translate into sensory impressions to reach the conscious awareness. This is why some trippers report seeing colors that do not exist, or hearing music of unearthly and impossible beauty. However, since it is a gross chemical disruption of the healthy functioning of the mind, it is extremely dangerous and completely uncontrolled. We would not drop a piece of tinfoil onto the live circuit board of a computer just to see what happens—neither should we drop acid onto our brains.

Those who took LSD harbored the notion that they had stumbled across something entirely new in the world. They were mistaken. Scryers have been deliberately manipulating their sensory impressions to access information that is not usually available through the senses for thousands of years. In that time they have developed many tried and tested techniques that yield specific, desired results. Since their actions are controlled and they use only natural substances and natural methods to achieve their ends, scrying is not dangerous. It is the original and best way to expand consciousness.

THE MOON IN SCRYING

In ancient times scrying was closely connected with the magic of the Moon. The lunar sphere is the lowest of the spheres of the planets, and for this reason the Moon was regarded as a kind of gateway between our ordinary, physical world and the mysterious realm of spirits. The Moon rules dreams, visions, hallucinations, fantasies, and memories—all functions of the astral plane, which exists one level removed from the physical plane.

The astral plane is not a place in space but another dimension of reality. It exists and penetrates our ordinary physical world the way music can vibrate on the air at the same time a human voice is speaking, or white light can simultaneously hold many separate different colors. The visions we perceive during scrying form upon the astral plane. This is also true of the images of our dreams, but when we dream we usually make no conscious inspection of our astral landscape. During scrying we remain consciously aware of what we see astrally, and are able to record our impressions.

Most of the substances used to aid scrying have historically been lunar materials. These include crystals, mirrors, water and other liquids, silver rings, lunar herbs, and hazel wands. It would be foolish to disregard this historical connection between the Moon and scrying. Wherever possible, lunar symbols and substances will be specified in this work, and lunar times observed, when recommending the best ways to use the various scrying methods that are described in Part Two. The reader may choose to observe this lunar connection or disregard it.

The Moon can become a potent ally for the scryer who understands and respects her changing rhythms. The power of the Moon is well known to witches who follow the teachings of Gerald Gardner, Sybil Leek, Raymond Buckland, and other great leaders of the modern Wiccan movement. The Moon has always been central to Wicca. However, her power has not been so well appreciated by practitioners of ceremonial high magic, or those who merely consider themselves psychic and want no part of the Old Religion. To disregard the Moon in scrying is to willfully reject the most useful of all symbolic associations.

CHAPTER 2

How Scrying Works

THE PSYCHOLOGICAL MECHANISM

There are many different scrying methods. Some of the traditional techniques will be examined at length in subsequent chapters. In the course of their practice individual scryers will modify aspects of the method they use to suit their own needs, or will invent entirely new techniques that work best for them. However, no matter how they may differ outwardly, all forms of scrying rely on the same basic psychological mechanism.

The scryer concentrates awareness upon some physical object, or uses a preset series of mental or physical actions, in order to bring about a receptive mental state capable of receiving information gathered by the deep mind.

Ordinary consciousness blocks the reception of this scried information. That is why it is so rare to get an extrasensory perception when we are engaged in our ordinary day-to-day activities. It sometimes happens that mediumistic or psychic individuals receive sudden visual flashes in their conscious minds, or hear mental voices issuing urgent commands. These clairvoyant or clairaudient episodes usually concern some matter of extreme urgency in their lives, such as the injury of a loved one or a fire at home, or foreshadow their own death or the death of a relative. They are not controlled, and so cannot be termed scrying. At times of extreme need the unconscious mind can break through or override the control of the conscious awareness to present important information obtained in extrasensory ways.

RECEPTIVE STATE OF CONSCIOUSNESS

Usually the need to present this information is not so great, or the unconscious mind is unable to break through the barrier of ordinary awareness no matter how urgent the need. This is where scrying comes into play. When we scry (no matter which method we use) we induce a receptive state of consciousness. We also instruct the deep mind that we are willing and prepared to receive information that has not been obtained through the avenues of our five senses.

If we do not specify a particular type of information, we may receive anything and will probably have a difficult time determining what it means. If we fix in our conscious awareness the specific area of information we are interested in getting before we start to scry, this instructs the deep mind to send us data in a very narrow range—the experiences of a certain person in history, for example, or the outcome of some future event, or the location of a lost person or object. A narrowly defined topic can yield more useful data, but it is also more difficult to access reliably.

SCRYING AND HYPNOTISM

It would not be correct to refer to the heightened or receptive consciousness of a scryer as a trance state, because the scryer usually feels no different while scrying, or at most experiences only a deeper concentration and loses a sense of the passage of time. A scryer can still talk and move and think normally while scrying. However, the mind of the scryer has changed in subtle ways that allow the perception of unconscious messages cast by the deep mind into images, sounds, sensations, or other sensory metaphors.

Scrying is really a form of auto-hypnosis. It is a mistake to regard a hypnotized person as asleep or unconscious. Hypnotized persons only appear to be asleep if the suggestion "sleep-sleep-sleep" has been given repeatedly during the induction process. The hypnotized subject will in this case follow the suggestion of the hypnotist and pretend to be asleep. If other methods of induction are used that do not rely on the imagery of sleeping, the hypnotized person will appear fully alert and awake while hypnotized, and will be capable of carrying on a perfectly lucid conversation with anyone.

During ordinary hypnosis the subject usually focuses his or her mind on some physical object and listens to the verbal induction of the hypnotist. The focusing of the mind lowers the barrier of ordinary consciousness to the input of the deep mind. The hypnotist tells the subject that he or she will listen to the words of the hypnotist and follow the instructions given. When these suggestions are accepted by the subject, the hypnotist is able to access the deep mind of the subject and call up old memories or forgotten incidents, or make the subject see or feel things that are not really there in the physical world.

THE POST-HYPNOTIC SUGGESTION

One of the most fascinating aspects of hypnotism is called the post-hypnotic suggestion. Even though it may take half an hour to hypnotize someone the first time, the hypnotist can re-hypnotize that same person in an instant by planting a post-hypnotic suggestion during the initial induction that the subject will enter a hypnotized state upon being given a simple signal such as a certain word or the snapping of the fingers.

While the subject is hypnotized for the first time, if the hypnotist tells the subject to return to the same hypnotized state upon hearing the hypnotist speak the word "cider," this will happen even if the subject has been out of hypnosis for days or weeks. When the hypnotist says "cider" the subject will usually not appear changed in any way, but he or she will have entered a receptive state of consciousness without being aware of it. The subject will unconsciously accept the instructions of the hypnotist as though these were his or her own ideas, no matter how absurd those suggestion may be.

For example, if the hypnotist meets a woman who a week earlier was hypnotized and given the post-hypnotic command that she will reenter the hypnotic state when she sees the hypnotist touch his nose, the moment he touches his nose she will fall into a receptive state without being aware of any change. If he tells her to lie down on the floor and wriggle like a

fish, she will do it. Then if he tells her to forget what
she has done and return to her normal state of consciousness, and asks her why she was lying on the
floor, she will have no idea how to answer.

If pressed for a response, she may make up some
absurd explanation to satisfy her own mind, saying
that her back was itchy, or that she just felt like being
silly, but in truth she has no idea why she lay on the
floor and wriggled like a fish because it was not her
own idea to do so, and she cannot remember receiving the command from the hypnotist.

WHAT HAPPENS WHEN WE SCRY

In scrying, we enter a receptive state of consciousness
that is very similar to the mental state of a hypnotized subject. The difference is that while we scry
there is no other person in the room to give us specific suggestions. Our mind remains open and waiting
to receive impressions. To some extent we can set the
parameters of this receptive state by fixing our consciousness on the purpose for which we are conducting the scrying session.

For example, we may hold in our mind that the
reason for the scrying is to learn the whereabouts of
so-and-so. This acts in the same way as the suggestion of a hypnotist that we will receive a certain sensory impression. Our unconscious mind is keyed by
our need to seek only information concerning the
location of so-and-so, and will gather that information
in nonsensory ways, translate it into sensory forms
that our awareness can understand, and deliver the
information to our consciousness as sounds, images,
and so on.

FIRST DIFFICULTY OF SCRYING

The scryer faces two difficulties. First is the attainment of a receptive state of consciousness. This is difficult for most persons in the early stages of practice but becomes much easier over time. Success breeds success. Eventually the mechanics of scrying serve to automatically induce this receptive condition, very much in the same way that a post-hypnotic command will automatically cause a previously hypnotized person to reenter hypnosis.

This occurs when experienced water dowsers pick up a dowsing wand. The wand in their hands automatically keys the necessary receptive state of consciousness in them without giving them any awareness of the change. They feel no different, but when they move over a water source that is picked up by their unconscious through extrasensory means, their deep mind directs their hands to turn the wand downward. To the dowser, the wand appears to actually turn of its own volition, and under its own power.

The picking up of the dowsing wand causes a dowser to enter a receptive mental state for the same reason that we all salivate involuntarily when we imagine a slice of lemon in our mouth. It is a conditioned response. The change occurs below the level of consciousness. Without conditioned response scrying would be extremely difficult or impossible.

The first time we take up a crystal ball to scry, little or nothing happens. As we continue to practice regularly, our mind gradually learns how to enter a receptive state, so that eventually we can enter a receptive state merely by uncovering the crystal and regarding it for a few moments.

SECOND DIFFICULTY OF SCRYING

The second difficulty faced by scryers is how to control and direct the subject of the scrying session. If uncontrolled, we might receive visions about anything. Since scried visions tend to be rather cryptic at times, it would be almost impossible to make sense of them because we would have no field of reference. For example, if we scry the vision of a horse stumbling and breaking its leg, we would be at a loss to know how to interpret it. But if we specify that the scrying session shall concern only our upcoming vacation, and we see the horse break its leg, we might interpret this to mean that there will be some problem or delay in our travel arrangements.

During regular hypnosis there is never any difficulty in limiting the impressions that are called forth from the deep mind. The hypnotist tells the subject to remember a specific event, or to witness a specific scene. Even though the visions that the hypnotized person sees may be cryptic, the hypnotist can be fairly confident that they relate to the area of interest in some way.

During self-hypnosis, and during scrying, which is a type of self-hypnosis, there is no hypnotist to give specific commands while the subject is in a receptive state. The trouble is, a mind in a receptive state of consciousness is usually incapable of giving itself instructions. By the very act of formulating commands in the consciousness, the mind leaves the receptive state, and the commands do not reach the deep mind.

This is very much the same thing that happens when we dream, and suddenly become aware that we are dreaming. For most persons, the moment they have the realization that they are dreaming, they wake up. The conscious state that allows them to realize that they are dreaming is incompatible with dreaming itself. It causes them to exit the dream.

SPLIT CONSCIOUSNESS

Fortunately, it is possible through strong desire and repeated practice to achieve a split consciousness that allows dreaming to go on with one part of awareness while another level of awareness becomes conscious that it is dreaming. In the same way, it is possible to achieve and sustain a receptive mental state during scrying, yet with another level of awareness to deliberately examine the visions or other impressions that are received from the deep mind. It is possible to direct the subject of those scried visions during the act of scrying them.

The way to do this is not something that can easily be described. It must be learned through repeated practice in the same way that riding a bicycle or swimming must be learned. This involves a process of trial and error. All that traditional methods of scrying can do is provide a framework and set of tools that have proven successful to other scryers down through the centuries.

THE TOOLS OF THE TRADE

Scrying does not depend on objects such as a crystal ball, or a black mirror, or a Ouija board. These are aids to scrying, nothing more. In themselves they have no power whatsoever. A skilled scryer can scry with nothing but his or her own mind. However, crystals and other tools have been regarded for thousands of years as helpful in scrying. They do not enable scrying in themselves, but they help create a favorable mental condition that encourages the formation of the necessary receptive state of consciousness.

Over time a particular object such as a crystal ball can, through conditioning, become the trigger or key that induces in a few moments the desired mind-state for scrying. This is what is meant when it is sometimes said that the tools of a magician acquire their power over an extended period of time. So also do the tools of a scryer acquire power for that scryer through repeated use. Unfortunately, these same tools will not have power for another person, since that person has not formed conditioned reflex patterns that allow those tools to act as triggers to induce a receptive awareness.

THINGS OF THE MOON

The traditional selection of tools for scrying was not a random process, but followed a very clear set of symbolic laws. Scrying instruments, substances, symbols, and times are those that relate to the Moon. While it is true that anything can be used as the focus for scrying—a rock, a stick, a nail—lunar objects and substances such as the crystal ball have been accepted by scryers down through history as more conducive to achieving success. It would be both arrogant and foolish to deliberately ignore this association between scrying and the Moon. True, you may still have success if you scry with a cantaloupe, but you are historically more likely to have success if you use a crystal.

The Moon controls the rhythm of the ocean tides and the monthly rhythm of menstruation in women. The instruments of visual scrying tend to be watery. These include water itself, ink, oil, rock crystal (which the ancient Romans and Greeks thought was petrified ice), obsidian, jet, glass, various watery gemstones, silver (which reflects images in the same way as the surface of water), and mirrors of all types.

WATER AND THE UNCONSCIOUS

Water is linked to the unconscious mind on the archetypal level. We might argue why this is so, but no one can dispute that it is so after the work of Carl Jung, who defined the primary archetypes of the human mind. In the myths of all the peoples of the world water is the realm of mystery and unseen forces. Since these forces were regarded as dangerous, water is the dwelling place for the dragon of chaos.

Water has the property of reflecting images. For primitive humans it was the only mirror. A mirror allows us to look back at our own faces. Naturally a mirror was regarded as a suitable instrument to look into our own unconscious depths. It is a window on the limitless sea of chaos, where all images lie latent and waiting to be revealed.

When we choose to use lunar materials for scrying, we access this primordial link between water and the unconscious mind. The use of rock crystal and other substances associated with the Moon predisposes the conscious awareness to become receptive, or reflective, to sensory metaphors created by the deep mind. This happens whether we wish it or not on a level far deeper than our reason. In itself it is not enough to ensure that we will have success when scrying, but it opens a channel between consciousness and the unconscious that greatly improves our chances for success.

CHAPTER 3

Who Can Become a Scryer?

SCRYERS ARE BORN *AND* MADE

Anyone with an innate talent for scrying can become a scryer. This includes a large percentage of the population. Perhaps as many as half the individuals in any modern city have at least a limited scrying ability, although in the majority of persons the gift for scrying is not developed, or even suspected, and lies latent all their lives. The only way to develop this gift is to use it.

The same is true of any talent received at birth. A great basketball player has the inborn potential to play basketball, but unless he or she practices long hours every day, this innate ability will never be fulfilled. An artist is born with the ability to draw, but this does not mean that all he or she needs to do is pick up a pencil and begin. At first the drawings of a Picasso will be almost as crude as those of any other child. The difference is that a Picasso will learn the art of drawing much faster than his peers, and he will

25

progress much further in a few months than they could progress in a lifetime.

You do not need to be Picasso to draw a picture. Neither do you need to be Nostradamus to scry. Not everyone who plays a musical instrument is a concert virtuoso. Not everyone who paints gets their paintings hung in the Louvre or the National Gallery. Not everyone who writes for a newspaper wins the Pulitzer Prize.

If you have a basic latent ability to send your mind into a receptive state of consciousness you will be able to get useful results when scrying. You may have to work much harder at developing your talent than someone with a greater gift, but this very labor will make you a better scryer at the end of the day than a person with a great gift who is too lazy to develop it.

HYPNOSIS AS AN INDICATOR OF POTENTIAL

One indication that you may have the talent to enter a receptive state of consciousness during scrying is the ability to be hypnotized. A small portion of the population—about twenty percent—can be hypnotized easily and at once can be made to enter a highly suggestible state of awareness. Another large percentage—perhaps sixty percent—can respond to hypnotic induction in some degree, but cannot be made to experience the full range of hypnotic phenomena. Then there is a third portion—around twenty percent—who resist hypnosis and effectively cannot be hypnotized.

Hypnotists agree that those who are hypnotized really hypnotize themselves. The hypnotist only provides a little guidance in the form of verbal suggestions. Anyone who can induce within themselves a suggestible state with the aid of a hypnotist can, at least potentially, create the same kind of mental state on their own without the aid of another person. However, self-hypnosis is more difficult than being hypnotized by another person, and requires a great deal of practice, effort, and concentration. The same is also true for the receptive or impressionable mind-state needed for scrying.

While it is true that as much as eighty percent of the population can be hypnotized by a skilled hypnotist to some degree, less than half the members of this group will be able to achieve useful results with self-hypnosis. The ability to induce a receptive state in your own mind and implant a suggestion is a much surer indication of a talent for scrying than is the ability to be hypnotized by another person.

A SEER OF VISIONS

If at some time in the past you have experienced a psychic episode of some kind, this may indicate a latent gift for scrying. Experiences of clairvoyance (seeing visions) or clairaudience (hearing voices) indicate successful efforts by your deep mind to communicate important information to your conscious mind.

Several or many spontaneous psychic experiences spread over a period of years are a better indicator of scrying talent than a single experience, which may be an anomaly triggered by a personal situation of extreme danger or need. For example, if you have seen psychic visions, ghosts, or auras on an irregular basis since your childhood, this is a surer sign of latent seership than the single, traumatic vision that the plane you were intending to fly aboard is going to crash.

The veracity of these visions is not important. When scrying, you will see and hear many things that have no correspondence in the physical world. You must learn to separate factual visions from symbolic visions. The key indicator is that your unconscious mind and conscious awareness are in communication with each other. Once this link is established, you can learn to use it to willfully access data that was acquired by your deep mind through extrasensory means.

A CHILD SHALL LEAD THEM

Children often possess a natural faculty for scrying. When they grow older they usually lose it. The cut-off age is around the time of adolescence—ten to twelve years in most individuals. Before this age, any child can create images in the air, hold conversations with a stuffed toy, evoke an imaginary friend, dream while awake or see monsters in the closet. When the child becomes a young adult the method for accessing the unconscious that was learned during play is forgotten.

In ages past, magicians and seers unscrupulously employed young girls and boys as scryers to take advantage of this natural ability. The magician would instruct the child, who was usually a boy of seven to ten years, to stare fixedly into a vessel of oil or a small pool of black ink held in his cupped palm.

The magician suggested to the child what he should be looking for, and instructed him to inform the magician the instant he saw it. The expected image might be something such as a flash of fire, or a column of smoke, or the approach of a man on horseback. When the child reported seeing the image looked for, the magician would record any scenes the boy saw and any conversations the boy might hold with spirits.

In effect, the magician induced a state of hypnosis in the apprentice seer and suggested certain parameters for the ensuing scrying session. However, the details of the various visions reported to the magician came forth from the deep mind of the child. They were not deliberately implanted by the magician.

It is highly unethical to subject a child to the consciousness-altering techniques necessary to scry, even if the child is aware of the procedure and willing to undergo it. Scrying is not dangerous, but to induce a receptive scrying state in another person through the use of fascination and verbal suggestion is to intrude upon that most private and sacred of spaces, the mind. Some astral visions can be frightening even to an adult prepared to receive them, but they can be absolutely terrifying to a young child. Everyone who scries should be allowed to make an informed, mature decision to do so on their own.

INDICATORS OF SCRYING ABILITY

There is no age or gender restriction on scrying. Many of the greatest seers have been men in their middle or late years. The water and mirror scryers of ancient Greece were often priestesses of the Mysteries, an indication that the ability is at least as strong in women as it is in men, and probably much stronger.

If there is a history of seership or second-sight in your family, this is a good indication that you have inherited a latent natural ability to scry. You may wish to have your natal horoscope examined by a professional astrologer for lunar influences. If the role of the Moon in your chart is strong, along with that of Mercury and Saturn, and if the sign of the Moon, Cancer, is prominent and active, this suggests a potent lunar current in your nature which may dispose you to clairvoyance, clairaudience, and other extrasensory perceptions.

Historically, it has been believed that some races are more gifted psychically than others. This probably has more to do with prejudice and superstition than accurate observation. Celts have long been thought to possess the gift of second-sight. The same is true of Gypsies. During colonial times in New England, Native Americans were associated with mediumship by the Pennsylvanian Dutch, a link that has survived down to the present in the cliché of the Indian spirit guide.

Even if it is true that certain racial groups have a statistically greater inherited ability to scry than others, this has no application on the level of the individual. For example, an individual Swede may well make a better seer than an individual Scot. Emanuel Swedenborg, a Swedish philosopher and gifted scryer of the spirit realms, demonstrates that no racial group is excluded from occult perceptions. Swedes would seem to be the least likely race to possess psychic abilities, if we follow the historical paradigm, yet Swedenborg was one of the most brilliant psychics who ever lived.

THE NUMBERS GAME

In his classic 1896 handbook *Crystal Gazing and Clairvoyance,*[1] John Melville reproduces a percentile table from Jacob Dixon's *Hygienic Clairvoyance* in which the scrying talent of the general population is divided into percentages for six progressively more profound levels of ability. Since it is so germane to our present topic, I will reproduce it below:

Percentage of persons who can become clairvoyant:
   63 in 100 can become Sensitives
   45 in 100 can reach the second stage of clairvoyance
   32 in 100 can reach the third stage
   14 in 100 can reach the fourth stage
   5 in 100 can reach the fifth stage
   2 in 100 can reach the sixth stage
In general:
   75 of 100 can become partially lucid
   56 of 100 men can become seers
   90 of 100 women can become seers

From my personal experience, Dixon's numbers seem wildly optimistic. I would put the percentage of those who can become what Dixon calls "partially lucid" at nearer to fifty percent. I tend to agree with him that more women possess an innate talent for scrying than men. However, many of the greatest seers have been men, not women. These distinctions may have more to do with cultural roles than innate ability.

Making an educated guess (and it is nothing more than this) I would say that forty percent of males can achieve at least a limited scrying ability, compared with perhaps sixty percent of females. By limited, I mean the occasional unclear perception that cannot be repeated at will. The percentages of those with advanced scrying potential are much lower—no more than about ten percent in men and twenty percent in women by my judgment.

In the final analysis it is desire coupled with regular practice that makes a scryer. True, there must be some basic ability to develop, but where this exists it is the determination to succeed that separates the professional working seer from the gifted amateur who experiences occasional visionary episodes, but has no idea where they come from or how to repeat them.

Chapter 4

Preparations

Practice Is Essential

If you seek to be successful when using the crystal or other instruments of deliberate seership, regular practice is absolutely essential. Each time you scry, you make a little stronger the conditioned reflex path that will cause your mind to automatically enter a receptive state. Once this reflex is fully burned in, merely gazing at the crystal for a few moments lifts the veil that obscures the interior of the glass and reveals visions. Scrying ceases to be an effort and becomes a joyful adventure.

To achieve this level of freedom, set aside an hour each day for the work. Night is usually the best time to scry because the night air is still and transparent, and at night the unconscious mind is nearer the surface. You may have noticed a change in your personality from daytime to nighttime. The nighttime persona is more emotional, more sentimental, more imaginative. You probably have not been aware of this change unless you keep a journal at night, or record your words on a tape machine shortly before going to bed. If you read what you have written or listen to your recorded voice in the light of day, likely you will be amazed at how sentimental and romantic you sound.

Ordinarily the difference between our day personality and our night personality goes unnoticed. To our own perceptions we are always just ourselves. Drunks do not realize how socially inappropriate their behavior is while they are drunk. Neither do lunatics (a word that comes from Luna, Roman goddess of the Moon) regard themselves as mentally unsound. Similarly, the transformation of our consciousness from day to night goes unnoticed by us, though not always by others, unless we make a record of our thoughts and feelings.

We can use this nightly transformation in our personalities to aid in scrying. Our emotional, romantic, impressionable night persona is much more suited to scrying than our pragmatic, cynical, controlled day persona. Even though the difference between these two sides of our nature is slight in those who are mentally stable, it is enough to facilitate the achievement of the necessary receptive mental state.

GENERAL GUIDELINES

You should not practice scrying too late at night, however. It is vital that your mind be alert. If you find yourself falling asleep over the crystal, nothing will be accomplished. Your unconscious mind will try to avoid the labor you seek to impose upon it by making you more sleepy than you would normally be, and if you are tired to begin with, you will drift into a stupor and end up wasting the period of your practice.

The rule is to scry at the same time each day for a set span of minutes in the same physical place. As far as is possible, all the conditions around you while scrying should be constant from day to day. Sit in the same chair. Face the same direction. Wear the same type of clothing. Follow the same general procedure. The purpose is to make scrying a conditioned response, so that when you perform a familiar and habitual set of outward actions in preparing to scry, the necessary mental actions over which you have less conscious control will engage automatically.

This does not mean that you must follow the exact same series of steps like some sort of robot whenever you prepare to scry. If, in the course of your practice, something feels awkward or wrong, the next time cut it out of your preparations. On the other hand, if while scrying you get the inspiration to do something new and it feels correct, continue doing it from night to night. In this way your routine of practice will not be static, but will evolve to suit your own needs over a period of weeks and months.

It is also important not to set too rigid a time limit on the sessions. Some nights you may wish to continue longer than other nights. There is no reason to cut a scrying short merely because your allotted time has ended. I recommend against keeping a watch or clock in the scrying room during your practice, or setting an alarm to let you know when your time is up. If you do these things, you will constantly be glancing at the clock or anticipating the alarm, and this will distract your mind away from the work at hand.

In addition to being wide awake, you must be in good health when seeking to access your deep mind. If you are in pain or have a fever, your physical condition will color the visions or voices you perceive during scrying and distort the information they convey. The images that arise in the crystal, for example, may become grotesque and frightening. If you receive clairaudient perceptions while ill, the voices are likely to be harsh and abusive, or even insane. Let your nightly practices lapse during those few days when you are seriously ill from the flu or other diseases. You can take up where you left off once you become well again.

THE IMPORTANCE OF DIET

It is a fact that a heavy diet of pastries, much red meat, fried foods, gravy, sauces, creams, chocolate, and junk foods such as potato chips and pizza will greatly inhibit your extrasensory abilities in all areas. No one really knows why this is true, but the general belief is that the physical body invests so much energy and attention in the process of handling and digesting these heavy, greasy foods that it drains a portion of the psychic vitality of the mind as well. Whatever the explanation, mystics have known for centuries that excess eating, particularly when the diet consists of heavy foods high in sugar and fat, poisons the extrasensory perceptions.

I am not advising that you starve yourself. Neither am I saying that you should suddenly change your diet in a radical way. Both courses are liable to do more harm than good. What I do strongly suggest, if you overeat or eat many foods high in fat, is that you moderate you diet. Cut down the amount of your usual portions. Try eating more chicken and fish in place of beef and pork. Cut out the junk food entirely.

Add more green and yellow vegetables to your meals. Do not fry your meat—broil it instead.

Above all, make sure that at least four hours have passed since your last meal before attempting to scry. Your stomach should never be distended, or still working to digest dinner. The last thing you want is to be listening to your stomach churn when you should be concentrating on the crystal. And this is exactly what will happen. During scrying the mind seeks any diversion to escape from concentrating on the task you have set it. This is not because scrying is harder mental work than other studies—it is only that the mind rebels against discipline. You should strive to eliminate as many obvious sources of distraction as possible before beginning each nightly session.

What you eat can be as important as when you eat. You do not wish to be troubled by stomach gas, heartburn, flatulence, or cramps. A food that periodically reminds you of its flavor hours after you have eaten it should be avoided. Also, be sure to go to the toilet well before you begin your session, or any of the preparations to your session, so that you will not have pressure in your bladder or bowel while your are trying to lift your consciousness to higher matters of the spirit.

These may seem like trivial concerns. They are not. The body does everything in its power to divert the mind away from spiritual pursuits. Usually we do not notice this distraction because we so seldom seek the spirit, but when we attempt to turn our attention away from our bodies, our bodies try equally hard to attract our notice. They behave exactly like a spoiled two-year-old when its mother is on the phone. You

will understand this for yourself as soon as you begin
to scry.

WHAT TO WEAR

To scry, you must be comfortable. Wear the same type
of clothing every night. This should be put on just
before beginning each session. A bathrobe is acceptable, or pajamas. If you scry shortly before going to
sleep, these clothes make practical sense. Otherwise,
you should wear clothing that is light, loose, and does
not irritate your skin. Tight blue jeans are definitely
wrong. So is a shirt or blouse that gathers at the
sleeves or collar in a constricting manner. Take off
your watch and other jewelry before beginning. The
exception is a ring that refuses to come off—this is
probably so much a part of your body that it will not
distract you during work. Do not wear shoes or a belt.
Loose slippers are acceptable.

It can be helpful to put on a special piece of dress
such as a robe or a headband or a cap that is reserved
exclusively for scrying and never worn at any other
time. Donning this ritual article will aid in triggering
the necessary receptive state of awareness. It should
be kept clean, treated with respect, and stored apart
from your everyday clothing. The same effect can be
achieved by putting on a special ring or pendant that
is only worn while scrying, and carefully stored in a
safe, secret place at all other times. How elaborate to
make your scrying costume, or whether to use special
garments at all, is a matter of personal taste. Ritual
garb can be helpful in separating us from our everyday reality.

RITUAL CLEANSING

If you have a shower each evening before bed, the time just after your shower is probably the best time to scry. The warm water will have relaxed your muscles. You are less likely to be distracted by an itch after bathing. Your sleepwear, which is probably comfortable and loose, makes an ideal working costume.

You may wish to speak a cleansing prayer during your shower or bath that is designed to cast off the cares and involvements you have acquired throughout the day. After you have finished washing yourself, but while you are still under the shower or seated in your bath, take a moment to close your eyes and recite these ancient words of cleansing that are drawn from Psalm 51 of the Old Testament:

> Have mercy upon me, O God,
> Blot out my transgressions.
> Wash me thoroughly from mine iniquity,
> And cleanse me from my sin.
> Purge me with hyssop, and I shall be clean;
> Wash me, and I shall be whiter than snow.
> Create in me a clean heart, O God;
> And renew a right spirit within me.

Direct this prayer to your personal deity, however you may conceive this being. As you speak this cleansing prayer, visualize all the cares in your mind and heart streaming from your body into the water. When you step out of the shower or tub, leave these cares behind you to be washed down the drain.

If this cleansing prayer seems too biblical or Christian for the magical work of scrying, you should find your own pagan prayer of purification that will accomplish the same purpose, one you can feel comfortable about reciting. I have given this prayer because it is the one I composed for my own ritual use and I know it is effective. A smaller part of this psalm was used as a prayer of cleansing by the Hermetic Order of the Golden Dawn for much of its ritual magic. The origins of the prayer are extremely ancient. It is probably based on the models of Babylonian and Egyptian prayers of cleansing.

For Wiccans and other pagans, I have composed a cleansing prayer to the Goddess that is based on the prayer which Lucius Apuleius speaks to the Goddess after immersing himself seven times in the waters of the sea.[2] Apuleius, the author of the celebrated *Golden Ass,* was a devoted priest of the Mysteries of Isis.

> Earth Mother, Queen of Heaven,
> Nameless Goddess of many names,
> Persephone beneath the stones,
> Artemis amid the groves,
> Selene among the stars,
> Wash from me my doubts and fears,
> Purge from me my daily cares,
> Cleanse my heart against my foes,
> Bathe me in thy celestial dew,
> Make bright the mirror of my soul.

If for some reason you cannot shower or take a bath every night, you should at least wash your hands and face shortly before beginning your practice session. As you do so, speak the cleansing prayer and allow your cares and preoccupations to run with the water down the drain of the sink. It is also a good

idea to brush your teeth. The cleansing of the hands
has traditionally been symbolic of the cleansing of
the soul.

CHAPTER 5

The Working Place

A ROOM OF YOUR OWN

A vital factor to success when scrying is the absence of distractions. You must have solitude, especially in the beginning when your are imprinting the conditioning necessary to access your deep mind. At the very least a private room is needed during the actual work sessions. In an ideal world this room would be set aside exclusively for your paranormal work, painted and decorated to be in harmony with your purpose. Life is seldom perfect. It is more common to make due with a corner of a room that is used for more mundane purposes during the day.

Even if you cannot have a work room all to yourself, you must strive to create a work space. Try to remove anything in the room that is bright or distracting, especially if it rests within your field of view while you are working. Unless you are using a mirror in your work, remove any mirrors or reflective glazed picture frames. Even if you are unable to paint the walls of the room a neutral color such as tan or pale rose or mist gray, you can use a tablecloth or placemat that is a plain white or neutral earth color. If the room you are forced to use has ugly curtains, turn your chair so that you are facing a blank wall while you scry.

FURNITURE FOR SCRYING

Any desk or table can serve to support the crystal, mirror, or other scrying instrument. It should have a space for your legs when you sit before it so that you can gaze directly down at its surface while sitting with your back straight. If the room you use for your practice sessions has no desk or table, a card table or occasional table can be used and then folded out of the way afterwards.

If possible, try to find a round table with three legs. The tripod recurs again and again in descriptions of classical scrying methods used by the Greeks and Romans, who always employed it to support the scrying instrument. Tripods had a mysterious significance for the Greeks. They were sacred and highly valued. When a Greek city-state made war against another city-state, the first act of the victor was to seize the tripods from the temples of the vanquished state and carry them home as plunder. The number three is a divine number, as expressed by the Divine Trinity that is found in so many diverse cultures.

The best seat is a simple wooden kitchen chair. This will tend to keep your spine straight and your mind alert. An alternative is an office chair or stenographer's chair. It is better if this has no arm rests, since it can then be pulled closer to the table. Your forearms will probably rest on the surface of the table in any case.

Some padding can be placed upon the seat if you are not accustomed to sitting for an hour in a wooden chair, but do not make it too comfortable. The goal is to find a middle ground between comfort and alertness. Any soreness or stiffness is counterproductive— but so is a slothful posture that will allow you to daydream.

SILENCE AND SOLITUDE

Regardless of how carefully you prepare and segregate the working space itself, if other persons or pets are in the house who demand your attention at all hours without warning, you will never be able to achieve the necessary degree of concentration. A barking dog, a squalling baby, or a well-meaning but intrusive mate can destroy an hour of effort in an instant. The apprehension that you may be interrupted can be just as bad as the actual interruption itself.

Try to pick a time for scrying when you are reasonably certain you will not be called away or distracted by external activities. Turn off the television. Unplug the telephone (or if you have a cellular phone, take out the batteries). Get rid of your beeper. Shut your dog or cat in another room, unless you are sure the animal will not make a nuisance of itself in the middle of your session. Let your husband (or wife) run after the baby for an hour.

Those who work at home while their spouse is at the office and their children are in school may find the morning or afternoon a better time for scrying. In this case it is best to draw the curtains of the work room so that the light will be soft and constant. This will also prevent you from being distracted by what is happening out the window.

SOUNDS AND SCENTS

If you spend a lot of time listening to music, you may want to play something pleasant in the background. It should be of the easy listening variety, classical or New Age, with no harsh changes. Do not put on a single music disc. It is certain to come to an end just when you are starting to concentrate properly. Put on several discs of the same composer or the same type of music that are guaranteed to run well beyond your longest practice session. Then you will not be anticipating the end of the music. Avoid vocal arrangements, or classical works that rise and fall dramatically in volume. Mozart is a good choice.

Incense can also be helpful in creating a special atmosphere that is associated exclusively with scrying. Cones and sticks are the least trouble, because once lit they sustain themselves and will smolder until they are entirely consumed. The more traditional powdered incense must be sprinkled over glowing charcoal and requires greater pains to prepare.

If you use cones, you must set them on a fireproof surface such as a ceramic tile or an ashtray. Be certain the burning cone will not roll off! It is not a bad idea to position this on the far side of the table at which you are working, or at least somewhere in front of you, so that you will notice if the incense inadvertently tumbles from its platform and ignites the carpet. Incense sticks are traditionally stuck upright into a shallow vessel of clean, white sand. This supports them and provides a non-flammable surface to catch any glowing sparks that may fall from their tips. Kitty litter makes a good sand substitute for cat lovers.

The rule for selecting the incense is the same as that for selecting music. It should be a type you like which is mild and not too intrusive. Rose incense is a good choice. So is sandalwood. If you find the scent overpowering after a while, or sickening, set it in another room or leave the window of the workroom open. You should be able to notice it without being distracted by it.

As an alternative to incense, you may prefer to light a scented candle upon your work table. A candle, scented or unscented, should always be lit just prior to beginning each session, and extinguished immediately afterward. The flame acts as a beacon for astral spirits who assist in the scrying. It is a traditional symbol for the fifth occult element, the quintessence of Spirit. Position it in a place where it will not dazzle your eyes or distract your attention away from your work. Be sure that it is long enough at the beginning of each session to last well past the end—you do not want it flickering out in the middle of your practice. This is both a distraction and an unlucky omen.

CARE OF THE INSTRUMENTS

Whatever special apparel, jewelry, instruments, and materials you use in your work should be stored in a safe place where they will not be disturbed by other family members or friends. It is best to keep them together in your work room, when this is possible. A small cupboard or chest makes an ideal storage place. Empty out anything that is not used in your scrying.

Always keep your instruments and materials clean and in good order. Even a carpenter or a mechanic follows this rule when putting away his tools—how much more should you follow it, when your tools are designed to penetrate the very fabric of time and space!

Always remember that what you perceive in the physical world is created within your own mind. If you treat your working instruments with respect and regard them as possessing a charge of esoteric potency, then they will indeed have power in your mind. If you handle them carelessly and throw them down anywhere you please, they will become objects of small importance in your mind, and you will never be able to get outstanding results from them.

THE ASTRAL PLACE

Just as your ritual instruments exist within your mind as well as in the physical world, so does your ritual place. The mental place of ritual, sometimes called the astral temple to distinguish it from the physical room in which the rituals are worked, is far more important for successful scrying than the material scrying chamber, because it is inside the astral temple that spirits and visions actually appear.

This is the most important truth of ritual magic, yet it is not well understood even by those who perform rituals for various purposes on a daily basis. The physical place is merely the ground or foundation of the astral place where you will do your scrying. The two are laid one over the other, like a slide image projected onto a painting, yet they are distinct. Spirits do not appear in the physical world (that is to say, in our mental perception of what we call the physical world), they appear in the astral world; but because this overlaps the physical, when we see a ghost or a vision in the astral, we tend to believe that it is materially present in the same way the chair we sit upon is materially present.

When we focus our attention on a material object, its shadow or ghost is created upon the astral world. Through repeated scrying rituals, the scrying room is projected upon the astral, and becomes perceptible to astral entities such as spirits. The more intensely we create the scrying chamber in the astral, the more easily spirits perceive it. They come to recognize the astral projection of the scrying place, and may enter it to communicate with us. To our perceptions, it appears that the spirits are present in the physical scrying chamber. In fact, they are present in the astral shadow of the physical chamber, which overlays the physical chamber like a slide image projected upon the furniture of a room.

It is important to understand the difference between the material scrying place and the astral scrying place if you are to grasp what is going on when you perceive elements of the scried vision outside the scrying instrument, as though these were present in the room with you, or you seem to be carried from the room to a strange location. This is a natural occurence in advanced scrying and need not be a cause for concern.

CHAPTER 6

Keeping a Record

THE SCRYING JOURNAL

As soon as you begin your daily scrying sessions you will want to keep a record of what you scry, and of the circumstances surrounding each session. The easiest way to do this is to get a good quality, loose-leaf three-ring binder and several hundred sheets of paper. You might also use a bound, lined copy book, but I prefer loose-leaf pages—if you make a mistake when you are writing in the information, you can always open the binder, remove the bad leaf, and start again on the next one.

Why would you want to keep a record? Unless you have a photographic memory, without a daily record you will forget the details of your visions, and in scrying there is much information concealed symbolically in the details. Even more important, you will never recall the circumstances surrounding each session that may have contributed to its success or failure.

Details of each scrying should be entered into the journal immediately after the session, while they remain fresh in your mind. Try to be as complete as possible. Even small details that seem to have no importance should be recorded. When you write down the vision or other perception you have received, do it in such a way that another person reading the record will be able to imagine the vision exactly as you actually perceived it.

DATE AND TIME

The most important detail is the date. Place this at the top of each entry along with the time of day and the duration of the session. Probably all your scryings will start at the same time, but some will go on longer than others. The date fixes each session in the context of the rest of your life. Years later you will be able to determine when you were having fertile periods and when your attempts were sterile. The date and time entry should look something like this:

Date: May 13, 1995
Begun: 11:00 P.M.
Ended: 12:37 A.M.

The date refers to the day the session was initiated. If a session begins at 11 P.M. on September 7 and ends at 1 A.M. on September 8, the date recorded would be September 7. If the session begins after midnight, record the actual day (which starts at midnight), not the day before. For example, if you scry on the night of June 17, but begin at 12:15 A.M., you would enter June 18 as the date. Once this convention is understood it eliminates confusion that might arise if the sessions begin just before or shortly after midnight.

PHASES OF THE MOON

There are several other very important factors that you should note at the top of each entry. These are the phase of the Moon, the weather at the time of the session, the humidity level, the air pressure, your physical state of health, your emotional state, and your mental energy level. Mental energy indicates your willingness to take on tasks and try innovations—your pluckiness, so to speak.

The Moon is marked on most household calendars in four phases: new, first quarter, full, and third (or last) quarter. The new Moon is shown as a black circle. The first quarter is shown as a half circle that opens to the left (its prongs point to the left), or a circle divided down the middle with its left side black. The full Moon is shown as a white circle. The third quarter is shown as a half circle that opens to the right, or a full circle divided down the middle with its right side black.

This is what you actually see if you look at the Moon in the night sky on these days. During the phase of the new Moon the sky is dark and empty because the Moon is close to the Sun on the other side of the Earth. During the full Moon the face of the Moon is a shining silver circle high in the night sky at midnight. It rises when the Sun sets, and sets when the Sun rises, so it is up in the sky all night. At the first quarter, halfway between the new and full phase, the Moon is directly overhead when the Sun sets, so it is visible during the early part of the night. At the last, or third, quarter, the Moon is overhead when the Sun rises, so it is only visible after midnight.

You can enter the phase of the Moon by the number of days after each quarter. In the case of the example given above, the phase of the Moon on April 13 of 1995 was six days after first quarter, which is the day before the full Moon. Since the Moon actually shows her full face on three nights (the night of the full Moon, the night before and the night after), we know that during this session the Moon was showing a full face and riding high in the starry sky.

THE IMPORTANCE OF WEATHER

Unless, of course, it was raining. Weather can have a profound effect on extrasensory perceptions and other psychic abilities, because it affects the way we think and feel. It is vital that you record the weather at the time of your regular practices so that you can gather information that will let you predict how well you will be able to scry under a given climactic condition. If you have easy access to a weather channel on television or detailed weather reports on the radio, or you keep your own local records, you should note the temperature, humidity, and barometric pressure, as well as whether or not the sky was clear, and what was happening—sun, rain, thunderstorm, fog, wind, and so on.

As you accumulate data, you will probably notice that certain weather conditions are better for scrying than others. In my own case, I find that I get the best results when it is raining, or just about to rain. Frequently during my most successful sessions the rain will begin to fall. This is accompanied by high humidity—a very favorable condition for the occult virtues of the Moon, which are essentially watery in nature.

PHYSICAL, EMOTIONAL, AND MENTAL STATES

When recording your physical, emotional, and mental state during each session you can be as brief or as detailed as you like. Under *physical* you might write something similar to: "Tired. Mild ache in left shoulder." Under *emotional:* "Variable. Nervous." Under *mental:* "Medium. Concentration wandered."

Another way to approach these personal records is to assign each a scale from one to ten, with ten being the highest, healthiest, and happiest, and one the lowest, sickest, and most depressed. The factors mentioned above would merit a 3 on the physical scale, a 4 on the emotional scale, and a 4 on the mental scale. Not a great day for scrying, but acceptable.

These additional factors are listed under the date and time in this form:

Lunar phase: First quarter, sixth day.
Weather: Clear and cool. Light breeze.
Temperature: 39 F.
Humidity: 46%.
Barometric pressure: 30.1 inches.
Physical state: Tired. Ache in left shoulder (scale: 3).
Emotional state: Variable. Nervous (scale: 4).
Mental state: Medium. Concentration wandered (scale: 4).

ADDITIONAL FACTORS

Depending on where you live, you may wish to enter the temperature in degrees Centigrade and the barometric pressure in millibars. This information is very useful when plotting performance graphs over periods of weeks or months. It can help you determine what conditions give you the best results.

Women might wish to consider entering the day of their menstrual cycle. Menstruation has been shown to exert a strong effect on the emotions and physical well-being of some women. The cycle of any periodic or recurring illness should also be noted.

WHAT TO RECORD

Only after you have established these general parameters for the session should you record a detailed account of the actual scrying itself. Do not bother to write down the physical procedure you go through when preparing to scry, unless it is the first time you are making an entry in your journal. These preparations will be the same from night to night.

If you begin to try some new approach or technique, or vary the usual preparations in any way, note the change on the day you initiate it. Similarly, if you cease to do some regular part of your preparations, note this change on the day you terminate the action.

Record the sensations you experience and the impressions you receive as you enter your receptive mental state. Write down briefly but completely what you see, hear, feel, smell, taste, or otherwise sense during the scrying. In the case of crystal scrying, this description will be similar to the description of a dream. It is quite possible to receive an impression through one sense avenue while you are scrying through another. For example, you may hear a voice speak a significant phrase while you are scrying for visions in the crystal. All these cross-sensory perceptions should be recorded.

MAKING A DREAM RECORD

It is also a good idea to make a complete record of your dreams during the period when you are engaged in nightly scrying exercises. These may be entered in your scrying journal, or in a separate dream journal. The dreams should be dated in the same manner as the scrying sessions. To get an accurate record of dreams, it is necessary that you place a pen and notebook beside your bed and record the details of each dream you can remember the minute you become conscious. If you wait until after you get up, most of the details will probably be forgotten.

This requires a certain degree of discipline. When you wake up in the middle of the night with a dream in your head, the last thing you want to do is turn on the light and begin writing in a notebook. If you just roll over and go back to sleep, the dream is lost. You must write dreams down at once.

THE ELECTRONIC RECORD

You may be someone who hates to write, or has difficulty expressing thoughts through writing. An alternative to the written journal is a tape recording of each session. This can be audio or video. Make sure you have enough tape to last longer than the longest possible session. Otherwise, you will find yourself thinking about the tape and wondering when it is going to run out. Those who own a stereo audio tape deck can plug in external microphones (one for each channel) and set these up on the scrying table. Alternatively, a dictation machine can be used that stops the tape between sentences. This avoids long silences on playback, but you may be distracted by the mechanical sound of the machine stopping and starting.

If a video camera is employed, it should be set up on a tripod and adjusted so that your upper body and the scrying table is in the frame, and placed near the table so that the built-in microphone can easily pick up the sound of your voice. These videos are likely to be tedious viewing, since they will be composed of long periods of motionless silence punctuated by a few brief verbal descriptions. External phenomena in the scrying room that can be mechanically recorded are unlikely. But if you already own a video camera you may prefer to go this route.

The drawback of audio and video recordings is that they require you to keep up a spoken narrative of what you are seeing and experiencing. This may not be possible if there are others trying to sleep in the next room, or if you are self-conscious about being overheard talking to yourself. Another shortcoming of tapes is that they quickly accumulate and take up a large amount of space. Remember, you will be doing a scrying each night. In a year that adds up to 365 tapes! You may be able to get two or three sessions on a single tape, but that still means a lot of storage boxes.

The Scrying Journal of Dr. John Dee

In a perfect world you would have a secretary sitting at your side during each session, ready to write down every detail you narrate. This is the method the great Elizabethan magician Dr. John Dee used to record verbatim the narrations of his seer, the alchemist Edward Kelley. Kelley would scry into Dee's crystal and report every detail that he experienced, both in the vision and externally in the chamber itself. He was a highly gifted seer, quite possibly the greatest of his age. While he spoke, Dee sat beside him and wrote down his words in a series of diaries. The result is an extraordinary record of crystal and mirror scrying extending over many years that has no equal in the worlds of psychic phenomena or English literature.

A portion (happily, the most important part) of Dee's diaries was published by Meric. Casaubon in 1659 under the typically verbose title of the day, *A True & Faithful Relation of What passed for Many Yeers Between Dr. John Dee (A Mathematician of Great Fame in Q. Eliz. and King James their Reignes) ...and Some Spirits.* This is usually shortened in modern times to *A True and Faithful Relation.* Recently the work was reprinted. Anyone seriously interested in scrying must study this record closely. It offers many practical insights into proven traditional techniques. It also illustrates the importance of keeping a continuous and detailed journal of all scrying sessions.

CHAPTER 7

Scrying Exercises: Basic

OPENING THE DOORWAYS OF PERCEPTION

The only way to learn how to scry is to scry regularly. However, there are certain mental exercises that can prepare the mind for scrying and make its achievement easier. These are most helpful for the majority of persons who have some latent scrying ability but are not exceptionally gifted.

We are accustomed to using only a limited portion of our mind and letting the rest lie fallow. Unless you are a graphic artist, you probably have not exercised your powers of mental visualization to any great degree. Yet you possess the ability to visualize images at an astonishing level of sophistication, as demonstrated by the clarity of the images in your dreams.

The same is true for all five of the external senses. By performing exercises to awaken these senses in our minds, we can facilitate the free flow of extrasensory information gathered by our deep mind and translated into sensory metaphors that our conscious

61

awareness can understand.

This set of basic sensory exercises should be practiced together as a regular routine at least several hours removed from your usual scrying sessions. Do not perform the exercises just before or just after scrying. If you scry at night shortly before going to bed, do the exercises in the morning or afternoon. They require no tools or materials, and can be practiced anytime you have a half hour or so of solitude. Look upon them in the same way that you would regard a set of physical exercises designed to develop your body. The same rules apply. They must be done daily and done properly if they are to have any useful effect.

It is better to do the exercise routine sitting up. When you lie down, it becomes too easy to allow your mind to drift. None of these exercises takes more than a few minutes, but during that time you must devote your full concentration to them. Most individuals will find it easier to do the exercises with their eyes closed.

EXERCISE ONE: A SIMPLE OBJECT

Imagine a simple physical object in your mind. The easiest way to do this is to gaze at an apple, a pencil, a key, or some other object close to you, then close your eyes and recreate it in your imagination. Try to make it as complete and lifelike as possible. Turn the object over in your mind and look at it from different angles, just as though you were turning it in your hand. Be aware of its color and texture, of the way the light gleams from its shiny surfaces.

You may work with the same object several days in a row in order to visualize it with the greatest possible clarity, but before you become tired of it, change to some other object. Keep the objects simple. Remember, there is no success or failure here. It is an exercise, not a test.

EXERCISE TWO: THE HUMAN FEATURES

Visualize the face and head of someone you know quite well. It may be the face of a family member or a relative or a friend. Stick with those individuals that you see on a regular basis. Examine the head from all angles, including the back. Study the ears, the way the hair hangs and curls, the lines above the eyes and around the mouth, the color of the eyes, the texture of the skin.

After you have a firm visual construction of the face, animate it in your mind. Visualize the person talking to someone as though you were watching a silent movie. Cause the face to smile, laugh, purse its lips, frown, scowl, become angry, look sad, and weep. Focus only on the image.

EXERCISE THREE: YOUR OWN FACE

This exercise is similar to the one above. Close your eyes and visualize your own face as you see it in the mirror every day. Study each of your features in turn until you have built up a solid composite picture of yourself in your own mind. Begin with the shape of your head, then move on to the position of your ears, the thickness of your neck, your hair, your eyes, nose, mouth. When one of your features becomes vague in your mental image, return your awareness to it and make it clearer.

You will be surprised to discover that it is much more difficult to hold your own face in your mind than the face of another person. It is best to do this exercise without looking into a mirror to refresh your memory. After all, you see your own face many times every day, so you know what it looks like.

EXERCISE FOUR: A FAMILIAR VOICE

Remember the sound of a familiar voice in your mind. It is best to begin with someone who speaks to you every day, but after you have practiced with familiar voices for a few weeks, you may begin to evoke the voices of more distant friends and relatives—individuals you may not have seen for months or years. The voice of a relative who has died makes an excellent subject.

You should cause these familiar voices to actually say the kinds of things that these people usually say to you. Have them use slang expressions they commonly use and recall the rhythm of their speech and their inflections. Recreate their tone, pauses, characteristic emphasis, and accent. Cause the remembered voices to laugh. You can make them say anything you wish, but it is more useful to stick to the types of things their owners usually say.

EXERCISE FIVE: SOUNDS OF NATURE

Remember in rapid succession the sound of a breeze in the trees, the gurgle of a rocky stream, the whine of a mosquito next to your ear, the crack of a twig beneath your shoe, the splash of a frog jumping into a pond, the rustle of your feet as you walk through tall, dry grass, the chirp of birds in the trees around you, the breathless whir of a hovering dragonfly.

You can vary these sounds from day to day if you wish, but try to connect them together into a single aural scene. You may want to recreate the sounds of a beach, or of a kitchen when dinner is being prepared, or of downtown traffic. Imagine the sounds alone as though you were present but blind, and forced to rely solely upon your ears to inform you about your surroundings.

EXERCISE SIX: TACTILE PERCEPTION OF SIMPLE OBJECTS

Imagine that you are blind, and that several small objects rest upon the table or desk in front of you. Mentally reach out and feel around for these objects. In succession you discover a tennis ball, a flat, polished beach stone, a coffee mug, a paperback book, a sharpened pencil, a paper clip, and a single leather driving glove with a snap at the wrist.

Pick up each of these objects and mentally turn it over in your hands. Feel the fuzzy texture of the tennis ball, the smoothness of the mug, the smallness of the paper clip, the softness of the leather glove. Riffle through the pages of the paperback. Feel the sharp point on the pencil. Lift the beach stone and estimate its weight. Spend a dozen seconds or so on each item before moving on to the next. Remember, you are blind, so you must feel for each item in turn and set it aside so that you know where it is.

EXERCISE SEVEN: OLFACTORY PERCEPTION OF FAMILIAR ODORS

Imagine in succession the smell of a rose, garlic, frying bacon, newly polished leather, a freshly cut orange, a cigarette, gasoline, vanilla, and burning hardwood.

You may change and vary this list as much as you like when these same scents become too familiar. It is not necessary to spend more than a few seconds recreating each smell, but you must be certain that you have actually evoked it in your mind. With practice, each odor will become as distinct as it would be if it were in the room with you.

EXERCISE EIGHT: TASTE PERCEPTION OF SIMPLE SUBSTANCES

In succession, imagine that you are tasting a fresh slice of lemon, a spoonful of white sugar, a block of chocolate, a peppermint, a stick of licorice, a piece of apple, a potato chip, and an aspirin.

When these substances become too familiar, vary them with different tastes of your own choosing. You can return to them anytime you wish to strengthen them in your mind and make them more real.

CHAPTER 8

Scrying Exercises: Advanced

EXPLORING THE ASTRAL WORLD

The following exercises involve abstract images or complex scenes of one or more senses. They require more time than the simple exercises, and should be done individually or in pairs when time permits. It is good to get into the habit of performing one of the advanced exercises directly after completing the standard routine of basic exercises. Devote anywhere from five to fifteen minutes to it.

Value in these exercises comes from the degree of sensory or extrasensory reality that is achieved, not from their duration. Nothing is gained by laboring over an exercise for an hour if its execution is faulty. This dogged determination to do the exercises at all costs will only cause you to loathe them, and cease doing them after a few short weeks. You will have better success if you do the exercises more times for a shorter period each time.

EXERCISE ONE: GEOMETRIC VISUALIZATION

Close your eyes. Visualize a tiny point floating in a featureless void. The void is neither light nor dark. The point is so small that you can't really see it, but you know that it is there. Direct your consciousness at it. Experience its smallness. The closer toward the point you extend your mind, the smaller it seems to become. You continue to move toward it with your consciousness, but can never quite get near enough to see it.

Stretch this invisible point into a thin line that extends infinitely in either direction through the void. You may visualize it as a fine thread with no more thickness then a strand of spider silk, but you should realize that, like the point, it has no real thickness and is invisible. Nonetheless, you can feel its straightness and its endlessness in both directions with your mind. Try to hold all of it in your awareness at once. This is impossible, because no matter how much of the line you hold in your mind, it always extends beyond the boundaries you have established.

Now go on to extend this line sideways infinitely in both directions so that it forms a plane that is invisibly thin and perfectly flat. Think of this plane as similar to the plane that lies between the perfectly flat surface of a lake and the still air above it. You can imagine it as an incredibly thin pane of glass, so thin that it really has no thickness at all.

Feel its thinness and flatness with your mind. Try to hold it all in your awareness at once. You cannot, because like the line that formed it, the plane extends forever in all directions. Keep expanding your mind in a vain effort to capture all of it for a few moments, until you have a real sense of its endless size. The edges of the plane always race outward ahead of your questing mind, so that you can never surround it.

Imagine a second plane that cuts through the first at a right angle. It too is invisible and endless, thinner than the film formed when two soap bubbles press against each other. These two planes divide all of the void into four identical parts. In your mind, move through the planes so that your consciousness inhabits each of these four zones of space in turn. Where the planes cross through each other, an infinite line is defined. Try to feel the equality of the four right angles that lie between the sides of the planes extending out from this line.

Finally, imagine yet a third plane intersecting the first two at right angles. Two new lines are defined by this third plane. They branch out from the single point where all three planes intersect, and in conjunction with the first line form six rays that extend endlessly away into the six directions of space: up and down, left and right, front and back. Contemplate the eight regions of the void defined by the three intersecting planes. Then shift your mind to the planes themselves, then to the three intersecting lines they create, and finally center your awareness upon the invisible point of intersection.

In this exercise it is important that you try to perceive these simple mathematical forms as things in themselves without giving them any qualities such as color, brightness, or thickness. This is impossible, but realize that when you visualize the point, the line, and the plane, in actuality they have no thickness and would be invisible to the naked eye. Try to feel or sense them as ideal forms rather than mentally see them.

EXERCISE TWO: SQUARING THE CIRCLE

Imagine a black dot on a featureless white background. Visualize it as the kind of dot you would make with a thick, felt-tipped marker on the page of a large drawing pad.

Draw a circle with your invisible magic marker around the dot in a clockwise direction so that the dot is in the exact center of the circle. Try to hold the entire circle in your mind at once without distortions or breaks in its circumference.

Mentally draw a thick, straight black line horizontally across the circle from left to right so that it passes through the dot at its center and divides the circle into equal upper and lower crescents. Draw another thick, black line vertically through the middle of the first from top to bottom to form a black cross with arms of equal length inside the circle. Hold this circle-cross in your mind for several seconds. Try to visualize it all at once rather than shifting your attention from one part to another.

Pull your mind back from the image slightly so that it appears to become smaller and draw a triangle around the circle so that the circle touches the middle of its three sides. The triangle is equilateral, with sides of equal length, and points upward.

Finally, draw a perfect square around the triangle. The base of the triangle forms the bottom side of the square. Notice that the triangle is not quite tall enough to touch the upper side of the square.

EXERCISE THREE: MEMORY VISUALIZATION

Recall in your mind a familiar and pleasant scene from your childhood. You might visualize the house you lived in when you were little, or a favorite toy you played with, or your earliest memories of the family car. You might want to re-create a walk through the hallways of your school, or your summer vacation cottage.

The best results will be achieved if you stick with one memory for several days, each day trying to make it more real and complete, then switch to something completely different and work with it for several days.

EXERCISE FOUR: FANTASY SCENE

Create in your mind a fantasy vision of something that you have never seen before.

For example, imagine that you are standing upon a hillside looking up at a white castle on the crest of a low, wooded mountain. See the pennants fluttering from the flagpoles atop the conical roofs of its corner towers, its tall gothic windows, its wooden gate. Observe the helmeted guards with their pikes held at the ready as they pace the serrated battlements.

Or you might choose to visualize a living dragon. See its sinuous coils and curves, its gleaming, iridescent scales and curved black claws, its golden serpent eyes and sharp white teeth. Watch it creep forward on its pale belly and rear up on its hind legs. Watch the blue and green fire fountain up from between its jaws like the jet from a blazing broken gas main.

EXERCISE FIVE: FULL SENSORY SUBMERSION

You are visiting the circus. Evoke the scene that is before you with all five of your senses just as though you found yourself sitting in the stands under the big top. There are clowns, acrobats, a juggler on a unicycle, a lady standing on the bare back of a white horse that canters around the center ring, elephants in the ring on the left, lions in an iron cage in the ring on the right, trapeze artists swinging high overhead. Everything is going on at once. You must turn your attention from one act to another to see them all.

Smell the popcorn and roasted peanuts and cotton candy mingled with the musty odor from the warm bodies of the spectators seated all around you. Hear the music of the organ, the beating of the drums, the voices and applause of the crowd, the trumpet of the elephants, the clop of the horse's hooves in the center ring, and the voice of the ringmaster booming out through the speakers of the electric sound system. Feel the summer heat and the beads of sweat that tickle your upper lip and trickle down your back between your shoulderblades. Feel the hardness of the bare bench you are sitting upon, and the vibration of the base drum in your chest.

The circus scene is excellent to revisit again and again. It is so complex that it will take you weeks or months to exhaust all its possibilities. Each time you visualize it, try to make it more real and complete. You should eventually be able to recognize the faces of the performers. Do not be surprised if some of them look your way and acknowledge your presence with a wave or a wink.

EXERCISE SIX: CREATING AN ASTRAL PLACE

Close your eyes and visualize your immediate surroundings. It does not matter where you do this exercise. Create your physical space within your mind and examine its details. Mentally look to each side and try to see exactly what you would see if you turned your head with your eyes open. Next, mentally look over your shoulder to visualize what is behind you. Turn your attention upward and re-create the ceiling or sky. Tilt your head downward in your mind and mentally visualize the floor.

After you have spent several minutes building this mental image, open your eyes and examine your surroundings to see what you have missed. You may want to close your eyes and add these missing features to your mental image of the place.

EXERCISE SEVEN: COMPLEX TACTILE PERCEPTION

Imagine that you are blind. Mentally walk around your house or apartment, feeling your way through the darkness. Be conscious of the cool tiles of the kitchen floor against your bare feet, the polished wood of your kitchen cupboards under your brushing fingertips, the smooth countertop, the metal of the refrigerator.

Move into your living room and feel with your hands the texture of your sofa and chairs, and the surface of your coffee table. Experience the carpet under your bare feet, the cool glass of your picture window when you lay your cheek against it, the rounded screen of your television, your curio shelves, and stereo system.

Move into the hall by touch alone and feel your way to the bathroom. Touch the shower curtain, the tiles on the walls, the sink, the back of the toilet, the edge of the tub, and the cold metal of the taps. Run some water over your hand.

Continue into your bedroom. Open the closet door by touch and feel your clothes hanging from the rod. Go over to your bureau and touch the familiar objects on its top. Open a drawer and touch its contents. Finally, sit down on your bed. Experience the texture of the spread and the softness of your pillow.

You may make this exercise as brief or as extended as you wish. Each time you practice it, concentrate on feeling the textures and shapes of a different room of your house. You may even wish to spend all your time examining a single piece of furniture or a single object. It is a good idea to actually close your eyes and move through your house by touch a few times to inform yourself of the sensations you will experience.

EXERCISE EIGHT: EVOKING A PERSONAL GUARDIAN

Sit comfortably and close your eyes. Create the inner sense that someone is standing a few feet away behind your chair looking down at the back of your neck. It is crucial that you do not use any of your usual five senses in this exercise. You must not hear the person behind you, or picture their image in your mind, or smell them, or feel the heat from their body. Try to sense the presence with your inner, sixth sense. Feel the prickle at the base of your neck where the eyes of the unseen visitor are directed. Experience the presence of the other person in itself, without sensory cues of any kind.

The presence is loving and protective. It watches over you as you move though the events of your daily life. It is constantly with you, your guardian angel who will help you to achieve a receptive state of consciousness and access your deep mind while scrying.

Project a strong emotion of love behind you into the presence and signal with this love that you acknowledge and accept the angel into your life. Imagine the angel stepping closer behind your chair to lay two hands lightly upon your shoulders. You should clearly be able to feel the touch and shape of these hands, and experience their warmth and gentle weight.

CHAPTER 9

Ritual Framework

THE PURPOSE OF RITUAL

In ancient times all forms of scrying or divination were accompanied by some sort of ritual structure. The power of second sight was deemed a gift from the gods. Usually scrying was conducted by priests or priestesses of the established temples. It was not a private recreation, but a very serious occupation. The fate of a city-state or even an entire empire might hinge on the pronouncements of a temple seer.

When communicating with the gods, certain ritual forms were always observed. These signaled to the gods that a vision was required and also did the gods honor and service. The relationship between a temple god of Egypt, Greece, or Rome and the priests or priestesses who attended upon it was symbiotic. The priests or priestesses nourished the god with prayers, devotions, offerings, and sacrifices. These gifts attracted the god and caused it to dwell within its temple image. In return, the god communicated with its worshippers, taught them secret matters, gave them visions and presages, and protected them in times of trouble.

Scrying was one of the ways the ancient gods communicated secrets to their priests. Other methods include spontaneous oracular dreams, inspired possession, lots, augury, and the auspices. Scrying was a sacred activity, not to be undertaken except by an individual who had dedicated his or her life to religious disciplines, and even then, only if that person was truthful, lawful, and of a noble mind and heart. If a man or woman polluted by vice, treachery, impiety, or other crimes attempted to scry, not only would the god turn its back on the offender, it would strike down the impious mortal with disease or some fatal personal mishap.

THE SECULARIZATION OF SCRYING

Today, scrying has become a recreation at social gatherings, or worse still, a cynical and predatory source of income. The role of the ancient gods is ignored. Most persons who use a Ouija board at parties do not believe in the existence of the very spirits who talk to them through the planchette. Since they approach this ancient and hallowed art with irreverent and carping minds, it is not to be wondered that the results they receive are trivial, mocking, or at times malicious. What kinds of spirits may they expect to attract, when their offerings consist only of snickers, sneers, and an attitude of contempt?

It is not necessary that we imitate all the steps of the sacred scryers of ancient Egypt and Greece to achieve useful and healthful results, provided that we understand the essential purpose that underlies these various rituals. To achieve the highest results when scrying, we must access that part of our deep mind that is concerned with spiritual matters.

ONLY STILL WATER REFLECTS A TRUE IMAGE

In magic, it is an axiom that like attracts like. As the Arab philosopher Avicenna put it: "When a thing stands long in salt, it is salt."[3] If we wish the spiritual part of our unconscious that manifests itself to our ordinary awareness as gods and angels and spirits for the purpose of communicating with us to come forth into our lives through the scrying instrument, we must make certain that the environment is harmonious for spiritual beings to inhabit.

We would not expect a fish to willingly visit with us on the dry, sandy expanse of a desert. Neither should we expect a spiritual being to make itself felt through a psychic atmosphere that is charged with doubt, desire, cynicism, arrogance, greed, and other low emotions that arise from the physical body.

To welcome spiritual beings into our awareness, it is necessary to make our awareness spiritual in nature. Since we are, by our very nature, incarnate souls living in vessels of flesh, this is an impossible goal that can never be fully realized. But we can try to the best of our ability to elevate that spiritual part of our own natures above merely sensual concerns and the desires and urges that arise out of the body.

ESTABLISHING A SACRED SPACE

With a ritual of preparation we create a sacred space around our self and the scrying instrument. A sacred space is an area of the physical world that has been defined and separated from the rest of the ordinary material universe in order to act as a temporary residence for spiritual energies. We conduct the ritual physically in the outer world, but also at the same time on the astral plane within out mind.

It is important to understand that your mind creates and holds the entire universe that you perceive and have perceived since the day you were born. Since the universe that you know lies within your own mind, you have power over it and can transform it in useful ways. One method for making transformation in your personal inner universe is ritual. It is a very ancient technique that has proven effective for countless centuries. It is equally effective in modern times, provided you use it properly.

There are as many forms of ritual for establishing a sacred space as there are gods, and more, since some gods are invoked by many different ritual forms. I intend to give a very simple technique that relies on what you have learned during your practice of the mental exercises in chapters Seven and Eight. To work it effectively it is imperative that you have gained some skill at creating astral structures through visualization. All of the exercises are designed to develop this skill, which is essential for scrying.

Preparations for Ritual

Always bathe, or at the very least, wash your hands and face just before you begin to scry. While you are washing, recite one of the cleansing prayers given earlier, or a similar prayer of your own composition. As you cleanse your outer body, strive also to cleanse your mind and heart and to make yourself tranquil and receptive.

Dressed in your scrying clothes, set your scrying instrument upon the table. You must handle all your scrying tools and materials with reverence. Never pick them up carelessly, or allow them to become soiled, or leave them lying about in the open after use. Scrying is a sacred activity, and these are sacred tools. They must be treated with the same attitude that a Catholic priest has when handling the host, or a Jewish rabbi feels when holding the sacred Torah.

Light the candle that symbolizes the radiance of spirit upon the scrying table. It will usually be placed on the far side of the table opposite your chair, so that it is behind the scrying instrument and well out of your way. Also light the incense and put on your scrying music, if you are employing these aids.

Sit in your chair before the scrying table with your back straight and your hands flat upon the table on either side of the scrying instrument. Close your eyes. Visualize the space around you.

The Scrying Ritual

CENTERING

Imagine a thin beam of white light extending down from the infinite distance above you to pass through the top of your head and out through the bottom of your chair. Try to feel its cool fire scintillating along the central column of your torso. The line has no ending above or below.

Holding this beam of light in your mind, imagine a second similar beam extending from the infinite distance on your left, which passes into your body through your left side just below your armpit and exits through your right side to continue forever into the distance on your right. Feel this beam flickering with cool fire in your chest. Notice that it intersects the vertical beam at your heart center—a spot in the middle of your chest between your nipples that is roughly on the same level as your heart.

While sustaining these two beams of light in your imagination, visualize a third beam that extends out of the infinite distance in front of you to pass through your chest and exits out your back between and just below your shoulder blades. It stretches endlessly in both directions and flickers with cool, white fire. Feel it within your chest. Notice that it intersects the point of your heart center.

PROJECTING THE SACRED SPHERE

Where these three beams of light meet, visualize a brilliant white star. Mentally expand this star into a pearl-white sphere of cool fire. Allow this sphere to escape the confines of your body. Continue to enlarge it until it surrounds your chair and scrying table. If you are using an entire room for your scrying, allow the sphere to fill the room. Parts of it will extend up through the ceiling and down through the floor, but this is unimportant.

As you project the sphere, speak this declaration of intention, either aloud or under your breath:

> By my act of will I establish this sacred space.
> The Light of Spirit creates it.
> The Fire of Spirit surrounds it.
> The Air of Spirit expands it.
> The Water of Spirit cleanses it.
> The Earth of Spirit sustains it.

When you have made this sphere large enough to contain your work space, sustain it in the back of your mind. From time to time as you carry on your preparations, remind yourself that it is still there and renew it within your consciousness through visualization. Even when you are not actively thinking about it or remembering it, you should know on a deep level that it continues to exist.

This sphere serves as your sacred space. Within it you may invoke spiritual energies and beings that could not easily tolerate the density of the everyday physical world. Think of it as a way station that is located halfway between the common material reality and the astral plane. Within it, you ascend from the sphere of the Earth to a level intermediate between the Earth and the Moon. Spiritual beings entering it to communicate with you descend from the sphere of the Moon.

These are merely mythic metaphors for what is essentially a psychological process, but they can be helpful in forming a practical model for what takes place within the sacred space. The gods and spirits who communicate with you within the sacred space are inhabitants of your own deep mind. You yourself (your memories and personal identity) are also an inhabitant of the universe of mind, but are a different kind of spirit than those beings we call gods or angels. They are bodiless or discarnate. You have a body of flesh and are thus incarnate. Stripped of your body of flesh, you would be made out of the same mind-stuff as an angel. It is our vessels of flesh that distinguish us incarnate spirits from discarnates.

INVOKING THE GUARDIAN ANGEL

It is common in traditional scrying to invoke the aid of a god or angel. If you are Christian, the best way to do this is to simply recite the Lord's Prayer or one of the psalms that is appropriate for your purpose, and call upon the presence of Jesus or one of the saints. If you are a pagan or Wiccan, you will prefer to invoke the Goddess in one of her lunar aspects. Selene, Luna, Artemis, Hecate, Ishtar, and Isis are all lunar goddesses.

As a more personal alternative, you may wish to invoke your own guardian angel. The Greeks considered the guardian angel, or higher genius (also called the good daemon), to be a spiritual being who remained with a human being throughout life, protecting and guiding that person, and, in times of extreme need, delivering prophetic warnings.

Some especially fortunate individuals were in

unusually close communication with their guardian spirits. One of the most famous of these was the Greek philosopher Socrates, who frequently received directions from his guardian genius in the form of what he called a "sign." His guardian usually made its presence felt when Socrates was about to do something that was not in his best interest. Whenever Socrates felt the sign of his guardian, he changed his plans.

Occasionally he was able to draw upon the extrasensory wisdom of his guardian to warn his friends when they were about to do something that would place their lives or fortunes in peril. He claimed that throughout his entire life up until the time of his death, the directing sign of his guardian had never failed him. For this reason he regarded his own death as a blessing, since, if it were a curse, his guardian would surely have warned him in time to escape it.

After you have extended the sphere of the sacred space and spoken its declaration of intent, regard the flame of the candle upon the scrying table and visualize a presence in human form standing several feet behind your chair within the sacred sphere. It is not necessary to invest this form with any physical characteristics. Merely sense its presence. If physical features or other sensory stimuli, such as the sound of a rustling robe or breathing, or the scent of flowers, occurs to you during this visualization, allow these things to become a part of your concept of this being, who is your own guardian angel or higher genius.

Do not turn your head or attempt to look at this being. You should not have a mirror or any shiny surface on the scrying table, because it might reflect the space behind you. This may cause your guardian to vanish, or make it more difficult than necessary for your guardian to manifest itself within the sacred sphere.

It is not by accident that so many fairy tales and myths concerned with unions between mortals and spirits stress the dire and sorrowful consequences that occur when the mortal seeks to steal a glance at the true form of his or her beloved. The spirit lover immediately vanishes, and all the gifts it has showered upon its mortal mate vanish with it. There is a lesson here for anyone intelligent enough to understand it.

If your guardian angel presents an image of itself to you in your mind, or within the depths of the scrying instrument, accept this image gratefully, but never try to search beneath its surface for a deeper truth. No mortal can bear to look upon the face of living spirit. It would consume the soul of the man or woman who tried. Rather than allow this, your guardian, who embodies the divine radiance of spirit within you, would immediately withdraw itself to shield you from hurt.

After you have built up a complete and sustained mental impression of the presence of your guardian angel standing behind your chair, mentally invite it to step nearer. You may find that you can hear the soft brush of its footfalls. Visualize it raising its hands from its sides to place them gently upon your shoulders. Feel the shape of your guardian's fingers, the weight and pressure of them, their warmth.

Speak the declaration:

By my act of will, I welcome the illuminating radiance of my holy guardian angel into this sacred sphere and into this temple of spirit.

CIRCULATING THE SPIRITUAL FIRE

From the hands of the angel, feel an energy flow into your body that is like a cooling liquid fire. This vitalizing force has many names in many cultures. It is the animal magnetism of Franz Antoine Mesmer. It is the Odic Force of Baron von Reichenbach. It is the chi of the Chinese Taoists. It is the mana of the Polynesians. It is the Kundalini fire of the Hindu Tantric yogis. It is the quintessence of alchemists and the occult virtue of medieval theurgists.

Allow the fluid fire to circulate throughout your body. Feel it rush along your nerves into your fingers and toes and make them tingle with vitality. You will discover that you are able to trace the course of nerve paths that you probably never even knew existed. Mentally direct the occult energy to concentrate itself in your third eye, the space on your forehead that lies just above the bridge of your nose between your eyebrows.

OPENING YOUR THIRD EYE

The Chinese sacred text *The Book of the Yellow Castle* refers to this as "the square inch field of the square foot house."[4] The square foot house is the human face. The square inch field is what is known in Kundalini yoga as the ajna chakra. It is linked with spiritual vision. Just as the physical eyes see the details of the material world, so does the third eye pierce into the secrets of the spirit realm.

Visualize an eye opening in your forehead between your eyebrows. The third eye is smaller than your physical eyes and stands vertically on its point.

It is roughly the size and shape of a large almond. Its left and right lids draw apart simultaneously to illuminate its orb with astral light.

Speak the declaration:

> By my act of will, with the holy fire of my guardian angel I open and illuminate my third eye of second sight.

When you see astral scenes through your third eye, you appear to see them through your physical eyes. This occurs because the extrasensory impressions of the third eye (which is a psychic, not a physical, organ) are translated into visual images that you are capable of understanding with your ordinary consciousness. Sometimes the information is given in the form of sounds, sensations, smells, tastes, or more vague impressions. Always bear in mind that in this process of translation, symbols and archetypes are used. These must be interpreted before the scried perception will make any practical sense.

CLOSING THE THIRD EYE

As you scry into the instrument with your higher vision, continue to draw energy into your body through the hands of your guardian as needed. When you conclude your session, visualize the closing of your third eye. When it is closed, speak the declaration:

> By my act of will, I withdraw the illuminating fire of my holy guardian and close my third eye of second sight.

RELEASING THE SPIRITUAL FIRE

Feel in your mind the occult fire that circulates in your body flowing out of your ajna chakra and withdrawing itself from your limbs. Feel it leave your body through the palms of the hands that continue to lie lightly upon your shoulders. Visualize it filling the unseen body of the angel behind your chair.

Speak the declaration:

> By my act of will, I release the illuminating radiance of my holy guardian angel from this temple of Spirit and from this sacred sphere.

Feel the hands of your guardian leave your shoulders, and sense the silent withdrawal of the angel as it steps back away from your chair.

ABSORBING THE SACRED SPHERE

Turn your attention upon the sacred sphere itself. Extend your mind until it surrounds the sphere and slowly draw it inward toward the infinitely small point of your heart center. Mentally locate your heart center by recreating the three intersecting rays of white fire. Contract the sphere until it is a brilliant white point of light in your heart center.

Speak the declaration of intent:

> The Earth of Spirit sustains it.
> The Water of Spirit cleanses it.
> The Air of Spirit expands it.
> The Fire of Spirit surrounds it.
> The Light of Spirit creates it.
> By my act of will I abolish this sacred space.

Extinguish the candle upon the work table, and put out the incense cone or stick, and turn off the music. With reverent care put away the scrying instrument and all other materials associated with the session. Then take out your journal and record every detail of what you have seen or otherwise perceived during the session.

PART II

Systems

CHAPTER 10

The Water Method
of Nostradamus

THE PROPHECIES

Water scrying, the most ancient of all scrying methods, was made forever famous by Michel de Nostredame (1503-1566), a French physician and astrologer better known as Nostradamus. He published an extensive set of predictions about momentous future events titled the *Centuries*. The first part was dedicated to his son, Caesar, in 1555.

The prophecies are written in verse and are ambiguous, making them very difficult to interpret, but they constitute the most significant prophetic writings since the Sibylline Books, which the sibyl of Cumae sold to the Roman king Tarquin the Proud (reigned 534-510 B.C.). It is a measure of the fame of Nostradamus that thousands of individuals still puzzle over and debate the meaning of his verses more than four centuries after his death.

A Subtle Flame

Nostradamus writes very little concerning his method of scrying. In a letter to King Henry II of France, he confides:

> I will confess, Sire, that I believe myself capable of presage from the natural instinct I inherit of my ancestors, adjusted and regulated by elaborate calculation, and the endeavor to free the soul, mind, and heart from all care, solicitude, and anxiety, by resting and tranquilizing the spirit, which finally has all to be completed and perfected in one respect by the brazen tripod.[5]

Elsewhere in the same letter he may make a veiled reference to his method when he writes: "Much as, if looking into a burning mirror we see, as with darkened vision, the great events...."[6] Nostradamus returns several times to the theme of fire when alluding to his scrying. This might seem strange for someone who divined in water, but the fire he means is not material fire but spiritual fire.

In the preface to his *Centuries* addressed to his son, he writes about prophets: "Although, indeed, now or hereafter some persons may arrive to whom God Almighty may be pleased to reveal by imaginative impression some secrets of the future, as accorded in time past to judicial astrology, when a certain power and volitional faculty came upon them, as a flame of fire appears."[7] A little later he writes: "For the human understanding, being intellectually created, cannot penetrate occult causes, otherwise than by the voice of a genius by means of the thin flame showing to what direction future causes incline to develop themselves."[8]

The "genius" he refers to is, of course, his good daemon or holy guardian angel. He describes the flame as "thin," meaning pale or rarefied. In medieval times the human intellect was thought to be composed of a very subtle, penetrating kind of fire. We can gain a better understanding of the nature of this spiritual flame by the description he gives when telling his son how he burned all his magical books:

> But dreading what might happen in the future, after reading them, I presented them to Vulcan, and as the fire kindled them, the flame, licking the air, shot forth an unaccustomed brightness, clearer than the light is of natural flame, resembling more the explosion of powder, casting a subtle illumination over the house as if the whole were wrapped in sudden conflagration.[9]

It is obvious here that Nostradamus is not really talking about his burned grimoires at all, but is intent upon conveying to his son the appearance of the spiritual flame that illuminates his vision during scrying. He considered this knowledge too sacred, and perhaps too dangerous, to set forth in an unambiguous way for anyone to read, so he veiled it within an incident of which the Inquisition could only approve. By the "explosion of powder" he means a bright white light similar to that caused by a flash of gunpowder. There were few other artificial sources of dazzling white radiance in the sixteenth century to which he could refer.

Two Mysterious Quatrains

There are two quatrains in the first Century (I.52,53) that represent almost all we know about the actual scrying method of Nostradamus. Although they are far from clear, I believe I have been able to decipher their meaning. Since the lost method of Nostradamus is likely to be of interest to all serious scryers, I will give them here:

> Gathered at night in study deep I sat,
> Alone, upon the tripod stool of brass,
> Exiguous flame came out of solitude,
> Promise of magic that may be believed.

> The rod in hand set in the midst of the Branches,
> He moistens with water both the fringe and foot;
> Fear and a voice make me quake in my sleeves;
> Splendor divine, the God is seated near.[10]

From the first quatrain we learn that Nostradamus scried at night and in solitude. He sat upon a three-legged stool, or supported his scrying basin upon a tripod—probably both. Tripods were considered sacred by the ancient Greeks, and were extensively used in temple divinations. The myths that exist concerning magical tripods that moved may have arisen from oracular tripods employed during scrying.

Apollo and Branchus

This first quatrain is clearly a direct reference to the method employed by the Greek oracle of Apollo at

Delphi, which is described by Iamblichus in his work *On the Mysteries*. The second quatrain is just as plainly a reference to the method used by the prophetess of the god Branchus, which is also described by Iamblichus in the same place in the same work.

It is worth giving the relevant passages here:

> But the prophetess in Delphi, whether she gives oracles to mankind through an attenuated and fiery spirit, bursting from the mouth of the cavern, or whether being seated in the adytum on a brazen tripod, or on a stool with four feet, she becomes sacred to the God; whichsoever of these is the case, she entirely gives herself up to a divine spirit, and is illuminated with a ray of divine fire....The prophetic woman too in Brandchidae, whether she holds in her hand a wand, which was at first received from some God, and becomes filled with a divine splendour, or whether seated on an axis, she predicts future events, or dips her feet or the border of her garment in the water, or receives the God by imbibing the vapor of the water; by all these she becomes adapted to partake externally of the God.[11]

The oracle of Apollo at Delphi was the most famous in all the ancient world. The priestess of the god, called the Pythia or Pythoness, was reported by classical authors to sit in a cave upon a small brass stool with three legs over or near a volcanic vent from which issued intoxicating fumes. The fumes caused her to burst forth in ecstatic poetry that foretold future events. No trace of this subterranean vent has been discovered at Delphi in modern times.

Branchus was the son of Apollo and a mortal

woman of Milesia. The woman dreamed that the Sun entered her mouth and passed out through her womb. When her child was born she named him Branchus (Greek: "the throat"). At a later time the boy kissed Apollo in the woods and became gifted with prophecy. His temple stood at Branchidae (later called Didyma) on the coast of Ionia. His priests, also called Branchidae, were reputed to be descendants of Branchus. The oracle of Branchus at Didyma was second in fame only to the oracle of Apollo at Delphi.

It is clear that Nostradamus is referring to the god Branchus when he writes of the rod set "in the midst of the Branches," that is, the Branchidae or priests of Branchus. However, this was not understood by scholars, who interpreted the "rod" to mean a pen, and the "Branches" to mean the fingers. "Water" was taken to mean ink, and "the fringe and foot" were thought to mean the top and bottom of the page. The quaking in the sleeves described by Nostradamus was assumed to signify automatic writing while possessed.

WATER SCRYING ACCORDING TO PSELLUS

This interpretation is all wrong, as the following passage from *De daemonibus* by Michael Constantius Psellus (1020-1105) demonstrates. Psellus writes at length about an actual method of water divination used in his own time. It is probably the same, or very similar, to that used by the prophetess of Branchus. The exact procedure was unclear even in ancient times because such sacred topics were not discussed openly:

Thus those about to prophesy take a basin full of water, which attracts the spirits moving stealthily in the depths. The basin, then, full of water seems in sort to breathe or move as with sounds; it seems to me that the water was agitated with circular ripples, as from some sound emitted below. Now, this water diffused through the basin differs but little in kind from water out of the basin, but yet it much excels it from a virtue imparted to it by the charms that have been chanted over it, and which have rendered it more apt to receive the spirit of prophecy.... When the water begins to lend itself as the vehicle of sound, the spirit also presently gives out a thin reedy note of satisfaction, but devoid of meaning; and close upon that, whilst the water is undulating, certain weak and peeping sounds whisper forth predictions of the future.[12]

This remarkable passage from Psellus appears in the works of Marsilio Ficino (1433-1499), who also translated and published the work of Iamblichus quoted from above. It is fairly certain Nostradamus read both Iamblichus and Psellus in Ficino's works, and that this source gave him the structure for his personal method of water scrying.

THE LOST METHOD OF NOSTRADAMUS REVEALED

The clue to what I believe to be the actual method employed by Nostradamus is given in Psellus by his emphasis on the sounds that issued from the scrying basin. We all as children (and sometimes as bored adults) have dipped our finger into a goblet of liquid and, by drawing our wet finger around the rim of the glass, have caused it to ring with a sustained, clear, bell-like tone. Benjamin Franklin actually invented a musical instrument based on this obscure principle of resonance.

The "rod in hand set in the midst of the Branches" is a pun. It evokes the method of the prophetess of Branchus mentioned by Iamblichus, but also is meant to signify a living, or green, wand—"in the midst of the Branches" means that the shaft of the wand *(virga)* was set in the midst of branching leaves. We can guess this because green or living wands played an important part in the prophesying of the ancient Greeks and Romans. Usually these were wands of vervain or laurel. Nostradamus probably used a laurel wand with most of the leaves removed but the green bark left on the shaft.

The drying sap that seeped from the wounds made by the removal of the leaves caused the bark to become slightly tacky or adhesive. Nostradamus, already possessed by his holy guardian angel, dipped his laurel wand into the water of the scrying basin and used it to wet the rim of the basin. The "fringe" referred to in the quatrain is the rim of the basin; the "foot" is the end of the wand. By drawing the wand gently around the rim of the basin, he caused the basin to resonate. This is the "voice" that made him "quake in his sleeves."

The primary tone of the vibrating basin would be accompanied by other harmonic tones that would persist for a few seconds after the wand was lifted from the rim. The action of the resonating basin would also cause circular ripples to appear upon the surface of the water, as described by Psellus, who says that the water "seems in sort to breathe or move as with sounds." The "reedy note" of Psellus is the primary tone of the basin; the much more important "weak and peeping sounds" are the harmonics. Psellus says that these secondary tones "whisper forth predictions." It is these secondary harmonic vibrations that are the "voice" referred to by Nostradamus, which he interpreted with the aid of his guardian angel, "the God" who is "seated near."

THE QUESTION OF THE PENDULUM

There are other possible explanations, of course. It may be that the basin was made to sound by the repeated impact of a brass ring suspended within its rim on a long, thin thread that was attached to the end of the wand held in the hand of the scryer. In this case, the basin would have been inscribed around its rim with Greek letters. Such a form of pendulum scrying was used by the ancient Romans (see Chapter Seventeen on the pendulum). It is significant that in Roman pendulum scrying, the ring is said to tap out lines of poetic verse in heroic meter "such as are called Pythic, or those delivered by the oracles of the Branchidae."[13]

However, I tend to believe that Nostradamus made the basin speak by drawing the wand around the rim to create a resonant tone and its harmonics (or perhaps simply a random vibration of the brass caused by the impact of the wand upon the rough rim of the basin) following the description of Psellus. It is very probable that he also saw visions within the basin, which acted as an articulate, or speaking, magic mirror not unlike the one described in the fairy tale Snow White.

Chapter 11

Water Scrying

The Scrying Basin

If you wish to emulate the method of Nostradamus, you must obtain a large, deep bowl or dish made from glass, brass, or silver. It should have a smooth and even rim. If you can find such a bowl set upon a short pedestal base, it will resonate more freely. Otherwise, you must elevate your scrying vessel to allow it to vibrate. This is best done with a low tripod of brass or laurel boughs (the traditional supports), but a small cushion will also free the bottom of the bowl and allow it to resonate.

You must do your own experiments to discover which bowl or dish works best, how much water you should have in it, and how you should elevate it to get the best sound. A deep, rounded bowl will generally yield up a more bell-like tone. A vessel of heavy, cast brass works better than one of thin hammered or spun brass. I have used a large Pyrex mixing bowl with a smooth, flat rim. This gives a remarkably strong tone with several subharmonics.

THE WATER

The water should be collected beforehand from a freshwater pond, spring, stream, river, or lake. Do not take water from a source that is stagnant or polluted. If possible, collect your water from a fountain or natural spring that is known to have supernatural properties. The ancient Greeks believed that nature spirits dwell in bodies of fresh water, particularly in springs where the water wells forth out of the ground of its own accord. In Europe many of these famous springs were enclosed with stone and made into wells or fountains. The spirits of elemental water, which Paracelsus called Undines, are particularly fond of human beings and very willing to form close associations with men and women who invoke and give offerings to them.

The water may be poured back into the storage vessel after you complete your scrying session, and used again, but you should discard it before it becomes cloudy or contaminated and collect fresh water. It is good to do this once a month at the time of the full Moon, and best to do it under the actual light of the Moon, so that the moonlight streams through the water as you gather it.

As an alternative, set a sealed vessel with your water out in the moonlight after you collect it. You should use a clear glass container so that the light of the Moon shines through the water for several hours. After it is charged with moonlight, wrap it in white linen or blue silk and put it away until you are ready to use it.

THE WAND

A branch of the laurel, or bay, tree was most commonly the traditional wand of prophecy of the ancient
Greeks, but you will also have good success with
wands made out of the hazel and willow (both strongly lunar trees). In place of dried tree sap or resin, you
may wish to experiment with a short length of surgi-
cal rubber tubing slipped over the end of the wand to
make it catch and vibrate on the rim of the bowl.

Dip the end of the wand into the water in the bowl
until it becomes thoroughly wet, then use it to transfer some of the water to the rim of the bowl, allowing
the water to trickle off the end of the wand onto the rim
while moving the rod in a clockwise circular motion
around the rim. If you have achieved the correct
degree of friction between the wet end of the wand
and the wet rim of the basin, when you draw the side
of the angled wand smoothly around the rim, pressing lightly downward, it should catch and slip very
rapidly in succession to produce a steady vibration.

If, as may happen, you cannot achieve the proper
degree of friction between the wand and the basin,
you may wish to experiment with the tip of the index
finger of your dominant hand (the hand we use for
writing). This is very effective in producing the necessary vibration in the bowl. If you use this method,
hold the laurel wand crosswise in your dominant
hand so that it moves over the basin.

THE METHOD

Water scrying should be conducted within the ritual framework described earlier. Project the sphere of light. Invoke your higher genius and receive its spiritual energy into your body to open your third eye. The third eye represents all forms of extrasensory perception, not just psychic vision, so it is necessary to open it in order to hear the voices of the Undines, or water spirits, that speak from the scrying bowl.

I am referring here to your true third eye, which is your internal extrasensory perception. The eye you visualize opening between your eyebrows is only a symbolic representation of this psychic faculty, which may or may not aid in the activation of your higher perception. Every time we scry successfully the third eye is always open, even if we do not symbolically visualize it opening beforehand.

While you produce the tone, regard the dancing, circular ripples on the surface of the water. Allow the tone of the bowl to lull your awareness into a receptive state. The air must be perfectly quiet. Late at night is the best time. In the predawn hours the air is not only quiet but absolutely still, allowing even small sounds to carry great distances. You must be able to hear the very faint harmonic tones that lie beneath the louder dominant tone of the bowl. Needless to say, you should not play music when using the scrying method of Nostradamus.

Periodically cease to move the wand around the rim, and listen to the harmonics as they fade into silence. Allow these secondary tones to draw your awareness with them into the depths of the water in the bowl. Look through these depths and beyond them with your third eye. The information you seek may come to you in the form of silent images rather than whispered voices.

Nostradamus likened the visual impression he received when looking into the scrying basin to that of a "burning mirror" in which he saw with "darkened vision." The burning probably signifies that the basin was filled with spiritual fire. The darkened vision likely means that the images were pale and indistinct.

THE PSYCHOLOGY OF WATER SCRYING

What you are really trying to do when scrying into water, or any other medium for that matter, is to temporarily lull the critical reasoning part of your mind into a receptive, passive state that will allow the agents of your deep mind, or unconscious, to present information gathered by extrasensory means to your personal awareness.

The process is very similar to what occurs when you daydream. Boredom brought on by inaction or some simple repetitive task causes your critical, reasoning faculty to temporarily switch off. This allows your deep mind to present fantasy scenarios or visions that are like waking dreams. In scrying you seek to duplicate that abstract mental state with the aid of a fixed gaze that is focused on some simple object (in this case, water) and a repeating, monotonous sound (the tone of the bowl).

You may wonder how voices can speak to you out of the harmonic tones of a ringing bowl. It is the same way that the clicking of the track under the wheels of a train, or the swish-swish of windshield wipers in a car begin to form into words when you listen to them long enough. The words come from your deep mind. The harmonics of the bowl merely provide them with a physical framework upon which they can build themselves into meaningful words and phrases.

WATER USED AS A MAGIC MIRROR

It is not necessary to use sound in water scrying. The wand may be set aside, and the water in the bowl employed strictly as a magic mirror for scrying visions. The term "magic mirror" can be misleading. You are not seeking an actual reflection in the surface of the water. This would interfere with the visions. Position the bowl in such a way that nothing is clearly reflected in the water. It is best to darken the room, or at least make sure it is illuminated by a soft light source. Shadows reflected in the bowl are distracting.

The best material for a scrying bowl that is used as a visual magic mirror is black glass. This kills all reflections in the depths of the water and gives the appearance of a deep, dark well. Clear glass or lead crystal is not such a good vessel for scrying images because the light of the candle tends to reflect and gleam from the edges and cut angles of the bowl. Silver or brass work well because they are opaque, and the inside of the bowl remains shadowed from the light of the candle.

From time to time, lean forward in your chair and blow gently upon the surface of the water so that it ripples. Visualize as you do so that you are blowing away a gray mist that obscures the depths of the water, even as the wind blows away clouds that veil the great mirror of the sky. Visualize the water becoming transparent and illuminated. Without mental strain, allow yourself to look through the depths of the water in the bowl as if through a clear pane of glass.

What you seek is not in the bowl. The bowl merely serves as a window upon the visions. You must mentally extend your psychic third eye beyond the bowl. This cannot be achieved in a purely material way by straining your physical eyes. It is a learned mental technique. It requires that you stare into the water with your physical eyes, but at the same time extend your astral vision beyond the water itself on a higher level of seeing. It is something similar to what you do when you look into your memory for a remembered image.

RHYTHMIC CHANTING

If you rock back and forth in your chair with your face over the surface of the water, you may find it easier to achieve a receptive mental state. Rock with a gentle, rhythmic action. You do not need to rock far forward. Rest your hands on the edge of the table to regulate this rocking motion. As you rock, you may wish to chant this incantation designed to part the veil of the waters:

Za-car'-ay, Zod-am'-ran;
Oh'-doe Sic'-lay Kee'-ah.

Although these words may appear strange, they form an extremely potent phrase from the Enochian Keys of Dr. John Dee. The Keys are invocations in the angelic, or Enochian, language that open various dimensions of reality. The words I have extracted are the actual power words of the Keys. When these words are uttered at the ends of the Keys, they cause the Keys to become active.

I have rendered the original Enochian words into phonetic English to make them easier for you to pronounce, and indicated the stress with accent marks. The exact transliteration of the words from the Enochian is Zacare, zamran; odo cicle qaa. In English these Enochian words mean: "Move! Show yourselves! Open the Mysteries of your creation." There are different opinions about how Enochian words should be pronounced. The form I have given lends itself best to this particular chant.

If you chant the Enochian words in a hushed whisper that resonates in your throat, and push your breath out more forcefully when you voice the stressed syllables so that your breaths touch and move the surface of the water in the scrying bowl, the incantation will prove more effective. In this way the power of the words will be transmitted directly to the water, which is the elemental medium through which you seek to communicate with your deep mind, and with the self-aware beings that dwell in its endless, shadowy depths.

For best results, synchronize the rocking of your body and the stressed syllables of the incantation so that you rock forward once for each word on its stressed syllable. Since the first two words have three syllables and the last three words only two, the effect will be to space out the final three words for stronger emphasis. The incantation should be chanted over and over until the scrying bowl becomes light and images form in its depths.

CHAPTER 12

Scrying in Oil

OIL SCRYING IN BABYLON

Thousands of years before Nostradamus first poured water into his scrying basin, the Babylonians were using clear oil for the same purpose. We know the general outline of the techniques they employed because some of their magic books, copied and recopied down through the centuries, have survived into modern times. These are written in a kind of shorthand by magicians for the use of magicians, so many of the details must be filled in from other sources. Nonetheless, the traditional Babylonian method of scrying in oil is remarkably well preserved.

Although I do not expect you to use these methods in your daily scrying sessions, they have a great deal to teach the modern scryer concerning the psychodynamics of the scrying experience. You should analyze them from this perspective, and consider why the ancients did what they did, and how their techniques relate to modern practices.

As I stressed earlier, it is both unnecessary and unethical to employ children for scrying. You will achieve far better results if you experience the sensory metaphors of scrying directly for yourself, without a medium. In modern magic we have dispensed with the barbarous practice of slaughtering animals, and we have also done away with the cruel exploitation of children. However, in ancient times children were used in this way, and I have felt it necessary to present the ancient methods accurately, as much as I detest this aspect of them.

THE PRINCES OF THE THUMB

A very popular technique was called the Princes of the Thumb. The magus anointed his scryer, who was usually a preadolescent boy, with olive oil upon the forehead and the thumbnail. The shiny nail became a magic mirror in which the scryer saw spirits—the princes of the thumb. One such ritual preserved in a Hebrew magical text reads:

> Take a young lad and make a circle in the earth with a knife, the handle of which is black, and prepare the nail of the right thumb until it becomes thin, and take four smooth stones and put them in the four rows of the circle, and put the mentioned knife in the middle of the circle and place the lad into it before the pillar of the sun and anoint his nail and his forehead with pure olive-oil, and the lad shall look well at his nail, and thou shalt whisper into his ear this spell: "True God, at his wrath the earth trembleth, and the nations are not able to abide his indignation; the right hand of the Lord doeth valiantly, the right hand of the Lord is exalted" [Psalms 118:15-6], I adjure you, princes of the nail, for the sake of the sea and for the sake of the

three lights that are in the universe, that you should
bring the king Mimon in this nail, and the queen shall
also come with him, and that his two servants shall
come and that they shall bring there two lambs, one
black and one white, and they shall slaughter them
and take off their skin and cook them, and that they
shall bring there three glass cups, and that the queen
shall come on a white she-mule, and they shall put the
table in the slaughter-house, and that they shall bring
there the book of the oath of adjuration; and tell them
that they shall eat and drink, and they will tell thee all
thou desirest. And when thou wilt desire that they
shall go away, the lad shall take off the oil from his nail
and from his forehead. And when he inquires of them
he shall adjure them with the book of the oath, which
he brought, three times the king and the queen and all
who are with them, also that they shall tell the truth
concerning everything that he will ask of them in a
manner that the lad shall understand it, and also that
they shall not do him any harm.[14]

The "four smooth stones" are to be set upon the
magic circle in the four cardinal directions. The knife
is probably to be driven into the ground in the exact
center of the circle. "Before the pillar of the sun" indicates the proper time for the ritual, early morning
before sunrise. The "name of the sea" is the Babylonian god Ea, god of the ocean. The "three lights" are
the Babylonian gods Sin, Samas, and Marduk, which
the Hebrew scribe did not feel bold enough to copy
outright.

THE PRINCES OF THE HAND

Another version of Babylonian oil scrying was known as the Princes of the Hand. This involved the use of oil mixed with soot to make a black paste that was smeared upon the palm of the hand. It acted in exactly the same way as the anointed thumbnail, as the following example shows:

> Take a new knife with a black handle and make with it a circle in the earth so that you can sit in it with a boy or a girl less than nine years old, and anoint the left hand of either of them with olive oil and the black soot of a pan, and warn them that they should not look outside the anointed place, and then whisper into his right ear: I adjure you in the name of BSKT, K Katriel, MI, Maeniel that you shall appear unto this lad, and you shall give him a proper answer to all that he asks for me, and all this he shall say three times. And the lad will see a man riding on a white mule or on a white horse, and he shall say unto him three times: Blessed be he that cometh in the name of the Lord, and he shall say unto him: it pleases me that thou shalt go down from the mule or the horse, and thou shalt command thy servants to bring a lamb, and he shall slaughter it and roast it and prepare the table for him to eat it, and he shall tell him everything three times. And after they [the spirits] have eaten ask your question. And if they lie thou shalt say three times: I adjure you in the name of Sansniel, Patchiel, Sakiel that you tell me the truth, and whisper also three times into the ears of the boy and also in his head SDI, SID, MSH, TRIT, RIT, and you will know what you desire.[15]

THE PRINCES OF THE CUP

The Babylonians employed yet a third type of oil scrying that was known as the Princes of the Cup. This involved coating the inside of a cup that rested on its side with sesame oil and using it as a concave magic mirror to capture and magnify the light of a candle that was fixed on its inner rim. Again, regrettably, as is so often the case with ancient forms of scrying, two young boys were used as mediums by the magician seeking information from the spirits of the cup. I will not give an example of this cup scrying, since the magic mirror will be treated at much greater length below in Chapter Fifteen. It employs the same essential ritual structure as scrying by the thumb and by the hand.

OIL SCRYING IN EGYPT

From Babylon, oil scrying made its way into the magic of the Hebrews and Egyptians. Perhaps the Jews carried it with them when they traveled from Babylon to Egypt. However it may have reached the valley of the Nile, Samuel Daiches states quite emphatically: "There can be no doubt that this form of magic came to the Egyptians from the land of the Euphrates."[16] He traces it as far back as 2000 B.C. in Babylon. The most complete examples of oil scrying are preserved in the Greek magical papyri written in Egypt between 200 B.C. and A.D. 500.

Minor details differ from one technique to the next. The bowl (sometimes described as a cup or saucer) may be ceramic or bronze or copper. In the ritual to Anubis described in detail below, it is a copper cup with the image of the god Anubis inscribed upon its inner surface.

Several kinds of oil are mentioned, including olive oil, sesame oil, vegetable oil, herb oil, and Oasis oil (perhaps palm oil). Sometimes the oil is poured directly into the empty bowl. At other times it is mixed half and half with water, which is added first. Occasionally only a few drops of oil are added to the water in the bowl.

The Method of the Egyptian Magician Nephotes

In a letter by the magician Nephotes to Psammetichos, the king of Egypt, which describes oil scrying in detail, four kinds of water (to be mixed with oil) are specified for four classes of divination. If you call upon the services of the heavenly gods (that is, the gods of the planetary spheres), use rainwater. If you invoke the terrestrial gods, use sea water. If you invoke the great gods Osiris or Serapis, use river water. If you call upon the souls of the dead, use spring water.[17]

The magician must prepare himself for the ritual by remaining pure for seven days. In his letter, Nephotes says that those seeking to scry in the bowl should attach themselves to Helios (the Sun). He says to go to the highest part of your house at sunrise on the third day of the month (that is, the third day of the lunar cycle), lie down on your back upon a clean linen cloth with a crown of dark ivy around your head, cover your eyes with a black band (the "black of Isis"—see Chapter Twenty-five), and wrap yourself up like a corpse in its winding sheet. Your head should be oriented toward the east. You then are told to recite a very long prayer to Typhon, god of the underworld, which I will not give here.

TESTING THE SCRYER

It was usual for the Egyptian magicians to employ a scryer, although it is often stated in the magical texts that the scrying can be done by the magician alone, if necessary. The method of testing the scryer is interesting for the insight it gives into the receptive state of mind that is necessary in any good scryer.

The magician speaks down into the head of the standing scryer the following formula of Horus seven times: "Noble ibis, falcon, hawk, noble and mighty, let me be purified in the manner of the noble ibis, falcon, hawk, noble and mighty."[18] He (or she) then waits for the scryer to hear an oracular sound. If the scryer hears something with both his (or her) ears, he is very well suited to scrying. If he hears only with his right ear, he is still suitable, but if he hears with his left ear, he is unsuitable and should be rejected.

The left, or sinister, side has traditionally been regarded as the side of evil. The evil daemon speaks into the left ear, and the bad angel is sometimes said to sit upon the left shoulder for the same purpose. The right hand is the hand of blessing or generosity and the left hand is the hand of violence or judgment. Arabs eat with the right hand and use the left hand to wipe themselves after the act of excretion. In modern times, the left hand is associated with masturbation. We are told that fraudulent and deceitful persons never let their right hand know what their left hand is doing. All this indicates the evil traditional associations of the left side, which are mostly superstitions.

SEVEN NEW BRICKS

An important part of the ritual furniture is seven newly made clay bricks whose bottom sides have not yet been moved from the ground where they were set to harden. Since clay bricks were set to harden in the Sun upon a bed of sand, their bottom sides are sand-covered. The magician is instructed to collect these after he has purified himself, taking care that they never touch the Earth.

Three of the bricks are placed side by side in a horizontal row in the scrying chamber with their original sandy bottoms downward. The other four are spaced in a vertical row, also set in their original orientation to the Earth with sandy sides down. Viewed from overhead, these seven bricks probably formed a Tau cross (the shape of a capital T) oriented so that its point of intersection, where the scrying bowl rests, is in the east.

Some rituals say to place the four bricks around the scryer, who, however, it is cautioned must not touch the ground. I believe that this is probably an error. However, where the bricks are placed around rather than under the scryer, it may be assumed that they are set in the four cardinal directions upon the magic circle. The circle would surround the magician, scryer, and bowl.

A burning lamp is set to the south of the bowl on the right brick of the three of the crossbar of the Tau cross, and an incense censor is put opposite to the north on the left brick, so that these are in line with the bowl. The bowl rests upon the middle brick. To the east of the scrying bowl, in a crescent that encloses the top of the brick cross, are set seven clean loaves of bread, and beside them seven piles of salt, as food offerings to the gods.

THE INVOCATION OF ANUBIS

Clear Oasis oil is gently poured down the inside surface of the copper bowl so that it does not become cloudy with bubbles. The oil fills the bowl. The oil lamp and incense censor are lit. A ball of incense is placed upon the glowing charcoal in the censor. This is compounded of a mixture of frankincense, beeswax, styrax, gum ammoniac, and dates ground together in wine to make a paste and pressed into a small sphere. A leaf of the Anubis-plant is placed upon the lamp. The Anubis-plant is thought to be stachys, or downy woundwart (Stachys germanica).

The scryer enters dressed in a white linen tunic. About his breast is tied a girdle or belt made of sixteen linen cords, four of white, four of green, four of blue, and four of red, that have been braided together into one band. The magician causes the scryer to lie down on his stomach upon a clean mat that is spread over the four bricks that form the vertical beam of the Tau cross. These are spaced in such a way that no part of his body touches the ground.

The scryer grasps the lamp in his right hand and the incense censor in his left. Eyes closed, he sets his chin upon the end of the middle brick that supports the bowl so that his face is only inches away from the surface of the oil. The magician completely covers the body of the scryer and the scrying bowl with a linen cloth.

After praying to the gods for success, the magician instructs the scryer to open his eyes. If the scryer sees nothing, the magician tells him to close his eyes again and proceeds to invoke the light with the following words:

O darkness, remove thyself from before him! O light, bring the light in to me! Pshoi that is in the abyss, bring in the light to me! O Osiris, who is in the Nesheme-boat, bring in the light to me! These four winds that are without, bring in the light to me! O thou in whose hand is the [present] moment, that [god who] belongeth to these hours, bring in the light to me! Anubis, the good oxherd, bring in the light to me! For thou shalt give protection to me here today. For I am Horus son of Isis, the good son of Osiris; thou shalt bring the gods to the place of judgment, and thou shalt cause them to do my business, and they shall make my affair proceed; Netbeou, thou shalt cause them to do it. For I am Touramnei, Amnei, A-a, Mes-Mes, Ornouorf-Ornouorf, Pahorof-Pahorof, Io, Little King, Touhor; let this child prosper, whose face is bent down to this oil; and thou shalt escort Souchos to me until he come forth. Setem is my name, Setem is my correct name. For I am Lot, Moulot, Toulot, Tat, Peintat is my correct name. O great god whose name is great, appear to this child without alarming or deceiving, truthfully.[19]

This invocation is spoken seven times over the head of the scryer, who lies with his eyes closed under the linen covering. Then the magician tells him to once more open his eyes. If he sees a light glowing within the bowl of oil, the magician encourages it with the words: "Grow, grow O light, come forth, come forth O light, rise, rise O light, ascend, ascend O light, thou who art without, come in."[20]

If the scryer reports that he sees the approach of the god Anubis, the magician encourages the coming of the god with an invocation, saying: "Thou art Thoth, thou art he that came forth from the heart of the great Agathodaemon, the father of the fathers of all the gods; come to the mouths of my vessel today and do thou tell me answer in truth to everything that I shall inquire about, without falsehood therein; for I am Isis the Wise, the words of whose mouth of mine come to pass."[21]

The magician assumes the identity of Isis, and of the other gods mentioned in his invocations, in order to acquire their authority. With this borrowed power he is able to command the coming of Thoth-Anubis and ensure that this god will speak no falsehoods. Isis is the goddess of magic. The strange names are barbarous names of power. These were frequently used in the magic of the Gnostic sects of Egypt.

The God Who Stands Up

The magician instructs the scryer to tell Anubis to bring in the other gods for a feast. When the scryer informs him that the gods have assembled, the magician invites them to partake of the bread and salt arrayed for them around the scrying bowl. Unless the magician is actually performing the scrying, he cannot talk to the gods directly, but must address them through the medium.

The reason the gods are given a feast, either provided by the gods themselves or supplied by the magician, is the general belief in ancient times that the spirits of the underworld did not have sufficient life force to speak to the scryer until they were fed. The feast infused them with strength. They did not eat the actual physical food, but the vital energy that was believed to reside within the food. Often fresh blood provided this nourishment, as in the *Odyssey* of Homer when the hero Odysseus feeds the shades of the dead with the fresh, warm blood of sacrificed sheep.[22] Blood sacrifice is not used in modern magic.

After the scryer tells him that the gods have finished their feast, the magician asks Anubis if the god is willing to answer his questions. If Anubis says yes, the magician says through the scryer: "The god who will make my inquiry today, let him stand up." If the scryer reports that one of the assembled gods has risen to his feet, the magician orders that the feast table be carried away. He tells the scryer to instruct Anubis to ask the standing god to reveal his name to the scryer, who then reports it to the magician.

Knowledge of the true name of the god that has arisen gives the magician the power to command his obedience. The magician proceeds to ask through the mouth of the scryer any questions he wishes the answers to, and the god who has eaten the bread and salt of the offering and freely offered his services must respond truthfully.

It is worth noting that Anubis, the jackal god, who is the form of the god Thoth that escorts the newly dead to the underworld, acts toward the other assembled gods in much the same role that is fulfilled by the scryer for the magician. Anubis is the spirit guide of the scryer, to use a term from modern spiritualism.

The scryer cannot communicate directly with the other gods, but only through Anubis—at least, until one of the gods has volunteered his true name, after which the scryer can address this god directly.

THE WISDOM OF THE ANCIENTS

There are many variations on this kind of oil scrying addressed to different gods with different magic formulae for different purposes. The ritual I have given above is typical. Usually such scrying rituals are not written out in this much detail in the magical books because it was assumed that those using them would already know the necessary practical framework. I have gathered information from several sources and combined it into what I regard as the essential pattern for this scrying method, which you should take some time to study and compare with the modern methods described in other chapters.

You can learn a great deal from the ancients, if you are willing to set aside modern preconceptions and seek to understand the logic behind their practices, even when these seem at first glance superstitious or silly. You will not go wrong if you bear in mind that everything the scryers of Greece and Egypt did was done for a purpose.

CHAPTER 13

The Crystal Method of Dr. John Dee

THE GREATEST MAGE SINCE MERLIN

John Dee (1527-1608) was the most remarkable magician to be born on English soil since the druid Merlin prophesied great things for Arthur Pendragon in his wars against the Saxon invaders. His father had been a gentleman server at the table of King Henry VIII. During the period when Henry's daughter Elizabeth was persecuted by Bloody Queen Mary and imprisoned in the Tower of London, Dee remained loyal to her. When Elizabeth came to the throne, she rewarded Dee by making him her court astrologer and personal advisor.

He turned the full radiance of his blinding intellect upon the dual purposes of acquiring arcane knowledge and helping to forward the expansionist policies of his beloved sovereign. Dee's private library was famous throughout Europe. He expended his entire personal fortune in acquiring printed books and manuscripts on all branches of classical learning and esoteric philosophy. As a young man he studied cartography under the master map-maker Gerhardus Mercator. Drake, Frobisher, Hawkins, and other great English navigators and explorers made pilgrimages to his home to consult him about the geography and inhabitants of distant lands that were little more than half-remembered fables.

THE SPIRITS CONTACT DEE

Dee hoped to increase the political power of Elizabeth, who at that time was in constant danger of being overwhelmed by the might of Spain and the malice of the Catholic Church, by enlisting the support of the angelic hosts. Through his studies he was well versed in all the magic of the ancient world. Mysticism and the occult held a lifelong fascination for him. In 1581 he became actively interested in spirit communication when for many nights he was troubled by strange dreams and unexplained knocking noises.

In his private diary Dee writes: "March 8th, it was the 8 day, being Wensday, *hora noctis* 10, 11, the strange noyse in my chamber of knocking; and the voyce, ten tymes repeted, somewhat like the shrich of an owle, but more longly drawn, and more softly, as it were in my chamber." These disturbances did not go away. In another entry he writes: "Aug. 3rd, all the night very strange knocking and rapping in my chamber. Aug. 4th, and this night likewise."[23]

It would be wrong to suppose that these nightly portents were the sole cause of Dee's scrying experiments, but they must have focused his attention powerfully upon the subject. He began to try to see visions within a small globe of natural rock crystal. On May 25, 1581, he records: "I had sight in *chrystallo* offered me, and I saw."[24] Despite this limited success, he soon admitted to himself that he lacked the gifts of a seer, and began to seek out a man with second sight who might take employment with him as scryer.

EDWARD KELLEY AND THE RED POWDER

Edward Kelley (1555-1597) came to Dee's hereditary home at Mortlake in the spring of 1582, probably seeking esoteric lore about the manufacture of the red powder of projection that would turn base metals into pure gold. He is fabled to have discovered a portion of this alchemical powder while on a walking tour through Wales. Usually he is said to have found it near, or in, the ruins of Glastonbury Abbey, but this is almost certainly a romantic embellishment of the tale.

It is also often said that he and Dee discovered the red powder together at Glastonbury. This story comes from the account given by Elias Ashmole: "Tis generally reported that Doctor Dee, and Sir Edward Kelly were so strangely fortunate, as to finde a very large quantity of the Elixir in some part of the Ruines of Glastenbury-Abbey, which was so incredibly Rich in vertue (being one upon 272330) that they lost much in making Projection, by way of Triall; before they found out the true height of the Medicine."[25]

From what I have been able to discover through my researches, Kelley already possessed the red powder when he took up employment as Dee's paid scryer. I find no evidence apart from this anecdotal account of Ashmole's that he and Dee discovered the powder together. The only certain thing is that he did have it during his stay with John Dee, and constantly sought to turn the angelic communications he received through Dee's crystal to the topic of alchemy with the hope that he might learn how to manufacture more.

THE ENOCHIAN ANGELS

Kelley had very little interest in the angels with whom he communicated through the crystal, except insofar as they were willing to lend him practical assistance in acquiring wealth and power. The angels treated Kelley with thinly veiled contempt and used him in much the same way we might use a telephone to reach Dee. Kelley always mistrusted the motives of the angels, but Dee accepted them at their word when they claimed to be servants of God.

Dee was frustrated in his effort to turn the revelations of the angels into political channels. The angels were largely uninterested in human politics. Their purpose was to convey through Kelley the system of Enochian magic. They were successful. Enochian magic is recorded in Dee's diaries, the most significant portion of which (as I mentioned earlier) was published by Meric. Casaubon in 1659 under the title *A True & Faithful Relation of What passed for Many Yeers Between Dr. John Dee...and Some Spirits.*

Although many books have been written about Enochian magic and John Dee, few attempt to describe the actual scrying method used by the two men in their angelic conversations. This method was delivered by the angels themselves during Kelley's early scrying sessions, and recorded in Dee's diary titled *Libri Mysteriorum.* For a more detailed description, see my book *Enochian Magick For Beginners.*

DEE'S CRYSTAL

The apparatus consisted of a small globe of rock crystal or, on occasion, a magic mirror of polished obsidian which Dee called, misleadingly, his "jet shewstone." Kelley mentions in his vision of the scrying table that the crystal rested within a frame. Dee sketched a frame in one of his diaries. It was golden with a small cross on top, encircled the crystal with a band, and had four legs.

THE SIGILLUM AEMETH

The crystal in its frame rested upon a complex seal called the Sigillum Aemeth (AMTh, the Hebrew word for "truth") that was engraved into the surface of a disk of beeswax. The angel Uriel gave explicit instructions about the exact size and shape of this sigil. It is, Uriel says, to be made of perfect wax, nine inches in diameter and somewhat more than twenty-seven inches in circumference, and in thickness between an inch and a quarter and an inch and a half.

The actual Sigillum Aemeth used by Dee and Kelley has miraculously survived through the centuries down to the present day, and resides in the safekeeping of the British Museum, along with Dee's other magical tools. Its front design consists of an interlocking pentagram within a circle, surrounded by a heptagon, surrounded by an interlocking heptagram, surrounded by a still larger heptagon, surrounded by a circle divided into forty parts. The whole is inscribed with many names of angels, letters, numbers, and small crosses. On the underside of the wax seal a circle-cross is engraved with the letters of the Kabbalistic name of God AGLA written in the angles.

THE SCRYING TABLE

The Sigillum Aemeth was placed in the middle of Dee's scrying table. As was true for the wax sigil, the angels give very explicit directions concerning the dimensions of this table. It is to be made from "sweetwood" and two cubits (around thirty-six inches) in all dimensions. Sweetwood is another name for the laurel tree. Its top is embellished with a border of Enochian letters. A magic square of twelve Enochian letters (3 X 4) occupies the center of the table. Around it is an irregular hexagram that extends to the letter border.

"A CLOTH OF SILK OF CHANGEABLE COLOUR"

The scrying table was draped with a white silk cloth that hung low so that it almost touched the floor. The Sigillum Aemeth was set upon this white cloth in the middle of the tabletop over the magic square of letters. On top of the wax seal was a silk cloth of "changeable colour" that hung over the sides of the table and had four tassels, one at each corner. "Changeable" probably means iridescent, changing from red to green as the light struck it from different angles. It was necessary to hide the sigil under the cloth because, as Uriel tells Dee, "This seal is not to be looked upon without great reverence and devotion."[26] The scrying crystal was set in its gilded or golden base on top of the wax disk that lay hidden beneath the silk. There is evidence that in place of this silk cloth Dee sometimes used a silk cushion as a support for the crystal. He laid this cushion directly on top of the Sigillum Aemeth.

SEVEN ENSIGNS OF CREATION

Arrayed around the central square on the table were seven talismans known as the Ensigns of Creation. The angels informed Dee these might either be inscribed on purified tin or painted directly onto the surface of the table. Dee painted them on the table. They were equally spaced in a circle so that they formed the points of an imaginary heptagram.

Each pertained to a different astrological planet and its hierarchy of spirits. Beginning at the top and proceeding clockwise around the table, the Ensign of Venus was followed by those of the Sun, Mars, Jupiter, Mercury, Saturn, and the Moon.

FOUR SEALS OF WAX

Dee's scrying table was placed in the middle of a red silk cloth six feet square, or four times the area of the table top. Each leg of the table was elevated upon a hollow disk of "sweet wood" into which was set a small wax seal. About these four seals Uriel says: "Within the hollow spheres [i.e. disks] thy seals may be kept unperished. One month is all for the use thereof." This seems to imply that these supporting seals must be changed for each cycle of the Moon.

These seals are usually said to be miniature versions of the Sigillum Aemeth, and this is probably the case. However an illustration of Dee's scrying table by the seventeenth-century occultist Dr. Rudd, which is preserved in a manuscript in the British Library (Harley MS 6482), shows four small disks around the table, each inscribed with a pentagram. Around each pentagram is written out in Latin letters "Tetragrammaton." The two disks at the top, or south, side of the table show inverted pentagrams. The one on the left has the Greek letters AL written in the middle of the pentagram; the one on the right contains the Greek letters PhA. The two disks at the bottom, or north, side of the table show upright pentagrams. The disk on the left contains in the middle of its pentagram the Greek letters OME; the one on the right contains the Greek letters GA. Alpha and Omega.[27]

These talismanic disks beneath the legs of the scrying table are interesting in view of the Egyptian practice of elevating the scryer upon four bricks. It was considered a profanation of the divine to allow it to make contact with the bare earth. Some monarchs of primitive cultures were carried their entire lives and never permitted to walk so that the ground would not defile their sacred natures. This, by the way, is the magical rationale that lies at the base of high-heel shoes. When a woman's heel is elevated from the surface of the earth, she is symbolically emphasizing that she is a living embodiment of the Goddess, and thus a suitable object for worship.

KELLEY'S METHOD OF WORKING

Kelley may have sat to the north of the table facing south. In Dr. Rudd's illustration of Dee's scrying table, the top of the table is oriented to the south, so that the central square of Enochian letters may be read from the north. However Dr. Rudd is not trustworthy as a source of information. Customarily, the scryer sits in the west and faces east across the bowl or crystal. Dee always opened each scrying session with a prayer, or prayers, to ensure that the angels who appeared to Kelley within the crystal, and often-times outside the crystal in the scrying chamber, would be angels of light.

Kelley sometimes felt a physical touch upon his head or shoulder at the start of the scrying sessions, as though some invisible presence were laying its hand upon him by way of introduction. The angels showed themselves to him within the crystal, caused scenes or dramas to appear in its depths, and spoke to him so that he clearly heard their voices. He also heard other sounds such as the crash of thunder and the crackle of flames. Even though he was using the crystal as a visual medium, during his scrying sessions all of his senses were engaged, and the images scried often extended outside the bounds of the stone itself.

Dee's method shows just how elaborate the furni-ture of a scryer could become. Its form was dictated to Dee by the angels themselves. This is the accepted manner for learning the details of any magical instru-ment or technique. Once the magician has succeeded in making contact with his or her holy guardian angel, the angel will describe in very precise terms exactly what is needed for success in future rituals. This is one of the reasons so many magical grimoires lack details. After contact is made with the higher genius, books of instruction become superfluous.

CHAPTER 14

Crystal Scrying

ANTIQUITY OF CRYSTAL GAZING

Crystal scrying is almost as old as water scrying. The druid Merlin is fabled to have used a crystal ball to peer into the future. The English poet Edmund Spenser describes Merlin's crystal:

> It vertue had to shew in perfect sight
> Whatever thing was in the world contaynd,
> Betwixt the lowest earth and hevens hight,
> So that it to the looker appertayned:
> Whatever foe had wrought, or frend has fayned,
> Therein discovered was, ne ought mote pas,
> Ne ought in secret from the same remaynd;
> Forthy it round and hollow shaped was,
> Like to the world itselfe, and seemed a world of glas.[28]

If Merlin did use a crystal ball, it was probably made of natural rock crystal rather than glass. Rock crystal has always been thought to attract and concentrate occult virtue. John Dee's globe, which he claimed to have received from the angels themselves, is rock crystal. Because of these traditional associations, you should try to get a ball of natural crystal if you can.

NATURAL ROCK CRYSTALS

Unfortunately, rock crystal balls are horrendously expensive. This is an inevitable consequence of the way they are made. To make a sphere of rock crystal, it is necessary to find a crystal that has a lateral dimension at least as large as the diameter of the sphere. The best rock crystals come from Brazil and, strangely enough, Arkansas. Good Arkansas crystals are as clear as water. Crystals can grow to considerable lengths. Six inches is not uncommon. But they seldom exceed an inch in thickness, so no more than one inch spheres can be cut and polished from such a crystal.

There are exceptions. The famous crystal skull supposedly discovered by F. A. Mitchell-Hedges in an ancient ruin in Central America was carved out of a single, near-perfect rock crystal into the shape of a life-sized human skull with an articulating jawbone. It is almost certainly a modern forgery, but is still a remarkable work of art. This skull is a huge semiprecious gemstone of very high quality. A similar skull of inferior crystal with a fixed jawbone rests in the safekeeping of the British Museum, and there are other crystal skulls, most smaller than life-size.

Once a crystal ball exceeds one inch in diameter, the price goes up exponentially. You can expect to pay thousands of dollars for a three-inch ball of rock crystal, and are not likely to get one without numerous cracks, bubbles, and discolorations. Flaws do not make a crystal unfit for scrying. All natural crystals of large size are likely to contain at least some minor flaws. However, flaws distract the attention during scrying and should be minimized where possible.

If you have a choice between buying a small, perfect crystal and a larger crystal with many imperfections, get the small crystal. It is a common mistake for beginners to believe that the bigger the crystal, the better it will work. Size has nothing whatsoever to do with scrying. In ancient times, as you have read, the Babylonians used the polished nail of the thumb for a magic mirror. It was also common to employ the rounded gemstones in rings, which were often polished en cabochon rather than faceted by Roman and Medieval jewelers.

GLASS CRYSTALS

The second choice for a crystal ball is good quality leaded glass. Since there is less constraint on the size of glass balls, you should be able to afford one that is four inches in diameter or larger. Buy it with a stand, if possible. Otherwise, you will have to make the stand yourself. This is a useful exercise for those with some craft skill. When you make your own stand, you infuse your own personal identity into it. This causes it to appear more clearly to spirits on the astral level, and helps to attract them.

As is true of rock crystal balls, glass crystals vary greatly in quality. When buying glass there is no reason to compromise. Look around until you find a glass crystal that is regular on the outside, with no sign of sag or ripples. You can easily see these defects if you turn it in a bright light and look through it. Avoid those that have numerous air bubbles. Also check for indentations or scratches on the outer surface. You should prefer a smaller glass sphere that it perfect over a larger one that has noticeable defects.

PLASTIC BALLS FOR A PLASTIC WORLD

The last choice for a scrying crystal and the least desirable is plastic. Plastic "crystals" are light, highly polished, perfectly round, and contain no flaws. They are reasonably priced, though usually not as inexpensive as glass. Even with all these factors in their favor, I do not recommend using plastic for scrying. It is neither a natural material nor an Earth material. Its occult associations are all wrong.

True, you can get excellent results with a plastic ball if you have a natural gift for scrying. But plastic is not a material that will focus and strengthen your gift. Plastic gives you nothing. It is very pretty to look at when displayed on an elaborate stand on the mantel, and may impress your friends. If this is what you want, buy plastic. A working crystal will never be displayed for casual view, and in fact will scarcely be seen by the physical eyes of the scryer during use. A working crystal is not a decoration but a tool.

Rock crystal has ancient links to the powers and mythic associations of the Moon. The Greeks and Romans thought it was a form of petrified ice. Even glass is linked to the Moon by its natural, earthy origins. It is formed out of silica, or sand, which is commonly found along the shore of the sea and constantly washed by the tides. Plastic is formed of complex carbon molecular strings and has its genesis inside Dow Laboratories. No lunar associations here.

"THROUGH A GLASS, DARKLY"

The surprising thing about using a crystal ball is that you do not actually see much of the ball during use. Crystal scrying should be done in near, or total, darkness. One way to accomplish this is through the use of a black or dark blue velvet cloth. This can be thrown over your head and shoulders as you bend close to the crystal upon the scrying table. Of course, if you scry at night you can simply turn off the light or blow out the candle that burns upon the scrying table.

Another approach is to build a black box of the kind my grandfather used. This must open on the top to reveal the crystal, which rests on the bottom of the box upon its stand. Line the box with black velvet or paint it with flat black paint. The enclosed space inside the box acts as a light baffle that eliminates stray shadows and reflections. For even greater security you may wish to drape a piece of black velvet over your head and shoulders, in a way similar to that used by early photographers. My grandfather stored this cloth inside his scrying box along with his crystal.

You may discover that you dislike total darkness while scrying in the crystal. Darkness is not essential. Edward Kelley, the seer of Dr. John Dee, scried in Dee's crystal by candlelight. A scrying box, or scrying hood, is still useful because it allows you to regulate the amount of light that reaches the crystal. The main thing you wish to avoid is reflections on the surface of the crystal. If there is a lamp or window reflected in the crystal, chances are that you will be distracted by its inverted image even when you try your best to ignore it.

My personal preference, for what it is worth, is to have the crystal very faintly illuminated by the indirect flame of a candle, so that I can see the light glowing softly within the depths of the crystal but not reflected from its surface. You can accomplish this by placing the candle behind you or erecting a small shield so that you cannot see the flame directly. I prefer to use a hood of white linen that covers my head and the crystal and allows the light of the candle to diffuse gently through.

How to Begin

When you begin to scry, focus your gaze upon the center of the crystal, not upon its surface. Try to look through the crystal as though it were merely a window upon the astral world. Probably the first thing you will see after concentrating your vision at the center of the crystal for several minutes is shifting gray clouds that billow and roll like thunderheads. These will begin to change color. Observe these color changes in a detached way but do not focus your attention upon them. Continue to scry through the crystal, not into it.

A white radiance that is similar to a milky mist will gradually spread outward from the center of the crystal. This will lift to reveal images. At first these will be very tiny and far away, but clear and unnaturally bright. If you focus your critical reasoning powers upon these visions, they will vanish at once. It is necessary to observe them with an absent mind and allow them to arise of their own accord. As you gain skill in scrying, it will become possible for you to focus your awareness more directly upon these images without causing them to be covered by the white mist.

This vital abstraction of the mind from the images that arise in the crystal is a learned technique. Once you begin to receive visions, you will quickly discover what internal mental actions you must follow to sustain them. Unfortunately, I cannot tell you exactly how to create the right mental climate for sustaining scried visions any more than I can tell you how to balance on one foot. You must try yourself, observe your mistakes, and learn by experiment. The correct mental state is the one that does not banish the visions.

THE METHOD OF MISS X

If you find, as often happens, that you are getting no results after half a dozen sessions, you may wish to employ the technique for training the mind to receive visions which was developed by Miss Goodrich Freer, who liked to call herself Miss X. She suggested that beginners should look around the scrying room and focus their attention on some small object, then close their eyes and mentally attempt to transfer the image of the object into the crystal, to be observed when the eyes are reopened. If successful, the next step she suggests is to transfer the image of some strong memory into the crystal and observe it in the same way.[29]

These exercises are practical and based on sound principles. However, if you have seriously and regularly practiced the sensory exercises described in Chapters Seven and Eight of the present work, you probably will not need these techniques, except perhaps to create a link between the images formed in your astral mind by visualization, and the physical crystal. You wish to train your unconscious mind to associate the concentration of sight upon the crystal as a signal that it should begin transmitting sensory metaphors that are localized upon the crystal.

COMMUNICATIONS WITH SPIRITS

If you scry for visions, sooner or later you are going to achieve communications with spirits. It does not matter what you conceive these spirits to be. You may think they are mere personifications of your own unconscious thought processes. You may try to dismiss them as illusions, or regard them as the souls of dead human beings, or alien life forms dwelling in another dimension. Probably all of these descriptions are wrong.

In practical scrying, it is not necessary to have a philosophical definition of spirits. It is enough to know that they will contact you, and that you can communicate with them mentally and through oral speech. If you seek their help, they will act as stage managers for your visions, and will help you to understand the meaning of what you have seen in the crystal. Whatever spirits may actually be, they behave as intelligent, independent individuals with their own personalities and purposes. You must treat them with respect and consideration if you hope to benefit from their presence.

Your own guardian angel, whom you should conceive as standing close behind your chair within the ritual sphere of light throughout the scrying session, will protect you from harm at the hands of other spiritual beings. Spirits have no power to physically cause you harm. However, if they are malicious, they can intrude upon your awareness with frightening faces in the crystal, and may cause you to have bad dreams.

THE PROTECTIVE ASPECT OF RITUAL

The main purpose for the ritual structure that surrounds your scrying sessions is to establish a very specific set of conditions within which you are receptive to scried sense impressions. After you have practiced for several months, you will find that you can easily see visions while within this ritual structure (specifically, within the sphere of light), but that you do not see visions while outside it. More than this, you will not even think about scrying or spirits while performing your daily tasks, but once you erect the ritual framework for scrying, you will immediately become receptive to the communications of spirits.

The ritual that surrounds your scrying sessions aids in the formation of a persona that only awakens within the ritual frame (this may be called the magical self). During your scrying sessions you become this magical self and gain the ability to perceive visions and understand the communications of spirits. Outside your scrying session your magical self is dormant. You do not really lose it, but it is asleep while you go about your ordinary tasks of living. You do not need to worry about the state of your magical self—it appears automatically when you have conditioned yourself with the exercises and used the scrying ritual, given earlier in this book, on a daily basis for several months.

THE SCRYER IS—"OUT"

It is very useful to make a clear division between when you will be receptive to visions and spirits—during your actual scrying sessions—and when you will not be receptive—the rest of your day.

You do this simply by not thinking about scrying or spirits during your daily routine. Occasionally a vision may arise, or a spirit intrude upon your awareness, while you are outside the sphere of light. Unless the information conveyed is extremely important, you should set it aside until your regular session. This division of personality accomplishes two useful functions. It makes you more receptive to visions and spirit communications while you are within your ritual framework. It also makes you less receptive to these same perceptions while you are outside your ritual framework.

SCRYING IN VIRTUAL REALITY

Once the crystal is activated, you may begin to receive impressions that seem to come from outside it. You will see visions in the air of the scrying chamber. Spirits will present themselves to you at the side of the table. This kind of total immersion experience is similar to computer-generated virtual reality, but far more real since it is not simulated by machines, but created by the mind itself. Often the spirits will appear to be smaller than human size. It is this psychological fact, so frequently commented upon by mediums, that accounts for the myths of fairies and pixies and elves of very small stature.

Another reality is that you will often see images

without being able to hear anything, even though the persons within the vision will be speaking, and you will be clearly able to see their lips move. You will sometimes perceive spirits only by touch, or smell, or by their disembodied voices. Sometimes you will see them only as quick, flowing streaks of light—like a falling stream of quicksilver, for example. Not all of your senses will be engaged simultaneously for every perception you scry.

HOW THE MIND SCRIES

When you think about what happens when you scry, you can understand why this is true. If a person stands in front of you and takes your hand to talk to you, that person reaches your awareness through whichever of your sense channels are activated. You see, hear, feel, and perhaps smell, that person all at once. However, when you perceive a spirit, it is not standing in front of you in a physical body. It communicates with your awareness through your unconscious mind by means of sensory metaphors that you are capable of understanding.

You perceive a pattern in your mind that you interpret as its form, perceive another pattern that you interpret as its voice, and yet a third pattern that reaches your awareness as the touch of its hand. Since these are sensory metaphors, not physical sense impressions, it is not necessary for them to occur simultaneously. You may very well feel clearly that a spirit is standing in front of you holding your hand, yet remain unable to see it; or you may hear it speak to you from close by, but be unable to see it. These sensory metaphors can, and often are, activated simultaneously for the complete range of human senses, but the point is that just as often only one or perhaps two sense avenues are activated.

LUNAR CHARGING OF THE CRYSTAL

You may find it useful to charge your crystal ball once a month with moonlight. On the night of the full Moon, after you have finished your usual scrying session, set your crystal ball in a window or out on a step where the moonlight can shine directly through it. To increase the effectiveness of this charging, place the ball into a bowl of clear glass filled with fresh water into which you have placed a pinch of salt. The salt water will attract the occult virtue of the Moon and transmit it into the crystal.

The crystal does not need to be charged every month, but you may wish to experiment with lunar charging on those nights when the sky is clear and the Moon is full, or close to full. Record in your scrying diary any differences this charging makes in your visions. It will not take you long to determine whether it is helping your work. If you detect no change in the performance of the crystal, you can either experiment with different charging methods or set the technique aside.

AWAKENING THE CRYSTAL—AN ANCIENT TECHNIQUE

A highly effective and ancient way to activate the crystal is to treat it as a living thing. Think of it as a spirit child. Each day, feed it with fresh milk, which you should allow to flow over its surface while you hold it in your hand over a bowl or the sink. Wash it with care and polish it with a soft, clean cloth. Talk to it in a loving and intimate manner. Kiss it affectionately. Whisper your secrets to it. Make up a personal name for it. Store your crystal amid fresh flowers and pleasing scents. Take it into your bed at night and warm it with your body while you lie asleep.

In this way you make the crystal a very desirable home for a familiar spirit, who will take up residence within it and will aid to activate its power when you scry through it. The familiar resident within the crystal acts as your spirit guide and helps you to obtain communications with other spiritual beings. It opens the crystal so that you can see visions.

If you think about it, you will realize that this is exactly the same thing that children do with their dolls. They talk to them and play with them. They cuddle the dolls in their arms and take them to bed at night. In this way a child infuses its doll with a resident spiritual intelligence that is perceptible to the awareness of the child. Children are not lying or pretending when they say that their dolls understand what they say. The method children instinctively employ to awaken their dolls is essentially the same that was used by the shaven priests of Egypt to attract the gods into temple statues.

JOHN DEE'S CRYSTAL FAMILIAR

John Dee and Edward Kelley had such a familiar spirit resident within Dee's crystal. It came to Kelley in the form of a little girl with golden hair and a green dress lined with scarlet. She called herself Madimi. This spirit behaved as you might expect a precocious

and intelligent ten-year old-girl to act. She treated
Kelley with a kind of witty good humor, as she might
behave toward an elder brother, and Dee with the
same deep respect she might show toward her father.
Kelley never trusted her, but Dee regarded Madimi
almost as his own spiritual child. In a sense she was
his child, since it was his earnest prayers and
thoughts that nourished her.

CHAPTER 15

Mirror Scrying

THE MIRROR OF NATURE

Mirror scrying is an evolved form of water scrying, just as is crystal scrying. In early times water was the only mirror. When it became possible to build mirrors that reflected an image, they were regarded as little dry pools—water that was fixed into place, so to speak, just as rock crystal was thought to be water that had petrified. The virtue of reflection was associated with the surface of water, so anything that duplicated this virtue must, by occult association, also duplicate the other virtues of water, one of which is the transmission of visions.

ANCIENT MIRRORS

Early mirrors were made of polished copper, brass, tin, marcasite (white fools' gold, which was known as the "mirror stone"), tin foil placed behind glass, mercury placed behind glass, obsidian, and polished silver, the most highly reflective element. Silver is the perfect mirror material. Its single drawback in ancient times was its tendency to quickly tarnish. This was not a problem if you were a rich Roman matron with slaves to keep your mirror constantly polished, but along with high cost its readiness to blacken prevented silver from displacing all other mirror materials.

Glass sheets backed with reflective coatings such as tin foil (tin pounded with a hammer until it was thinner than paper) or sealed pools of liquid mercury were not popular among the ancients because clear glass was unobtainable. Glass mirrors always appeared discolored or cloudy no matter how good the reflective substance that backed them. Obsidian, a black form of glass that occurs naturally, avoided this problem by reflecting light from its polished surface, but it gave back a very dark image that caused colors to appear washed out. It was unflattering to a woman's complexion, and so not very popular.

CHOOSING YOUR SCRYING MIRROR

All types of mirrors can be successfully used for scrying. A scrying mirror does not need to be large. A hand mirror, or even the mirror from a woman's compact or the side mirror from a car work well. Size is not important unless you intend to use the mirror as an astral doorway, and then you may prefer a full-length wall mirror that you can step into with your astral body.

Mirrors are naturally linked to the Moon. All modern mirrors are backed with silver, which is the lunar metal. All are made of glass, a lunar substance. All reflect images, a lunar property. There are several other associations that you can choose in order to make this link between your magic mirror and the Moon even stronger. If possible, use a round or oval mirror for scrying rather than a square mirror. The round shape is more in harmony with the full Moon. The best material for the frame of a scrying mirror is silver. If you can find a small round or oval silver picture frame into which you can insert a mirror in place of its protective glass, you will have an ideal scrying mirror.

Old mirrors seem to work better than new mirrors. Perhaps this is due to their romantic associations. Or it may be the result of the years and years of images they have reflected. Antique shops are excellent places to search for your scrying mirror. You will often discover an old cosmetic or shaving mirror that is slightly tarnished for a very low price. The tarnish does not inhibit the use of the mirror for scrying. The most important test is whether the mirror feels right to you when you hold it in your hands, and whether it stirs any intuitive response within you. If you listen attentively, your scrying mirror will call to you when you find it.

MAKING A BLACK MIRROR

Although you can use an ordinary mirror for scrying, it is easy to become distracted by the reflected image. Most seers prefer to use a black mirror that is specifically created for magic. Since you cannot (so far as I know) go into a store and buy a black mirror, it is necessary to make it. This is not really difficult. You will need only a piece of glass and a frame to hold it. Any frame for a photograph can be turned into a black mirror.

Take the glass out of your picture frame and paint one side of it with black enamel. You will probably have to use two or three coats in order to make the paint completely opaque. Oil-based enamels are more durable, but they require a long time to dry.

Be sure to leave the glass until the paint is completely dry and hardened before returning it to its frame. You may have to allow it to dry two or even three days after giving it the final coat of paint. When you insert it into its frame, put it in with the glass side facing outward. If you have taken care to remove any hairs, dust, or lint from the glass before painting it, you will have made a perfect black mirror.

The advantage of a black mirror is that it reflects less light, and therefore is less distracting to the eye. It gives the gaze nothing to fix upon. This draws the awareness of the scryer into it, as though it were a midnight well of water. Silver mirrors have the drawback that they are designed to reflect images as brightly and clearly as possible. The scryer does not seek reflections, but visions. For this purpose, the black mirror is a superior tool.

NATURAL BLACK MIRRORS

The use of black mirrors is many centuries old. Dr. John Dee employed a mirror of obsidian in addition to his globe of rock crystal. Dee's mirror is in the shape of a thick, flat disk with a very short handle that has a hole bored through it. As I mentioned above, obsidian was used by the Romans for everyday mirrors, but had limited popularity due to its shadowy reflections. This very property makes it ideal for a black mirror. Obsidian is a semi-transparent form of volcanic glass that ranges in color from dark brown to black.

The other traditional substance for black mirrors is jet, a type of polished coal. It is very similar in feel to amber, but black and completely opaque. Like amber, it attracts bits of straw and dust when rubbed with a cloth. Its natural electrical property makes it highly desirable as an instrument for scrying, because electricity has long been associated with psychic ability.

You may be able to obtain a slice of obsidian the size of your hand from a jewelry maker or craft supplier. Obsidian is used by jewelers as a semiprecious stone in the making of earrings, pendants, and so on. The jeweler cuts the size and shape needed for a project from a larger sheet.

If you are fortunate enough to find a sheet of obsidian, you will have to polish it or have it polished, and cut it or have it cut to fit into a small frame, which ideally should be made of pure silver. Ordinary obsidian of as dark a color as you can find is the best type. Banded obsidian, although more prized for jewelry, is not so good for a magic mirror. It consists of alternating bands of black and clear glass.

As an alternative to jet and obsidian, you may be able to locate a shallow bowl or plate that is made out of artificial black glass. This will work provided the bowl has a regularly curved surface without scratches. Use your imagination when looking for your black mirror. A witch friend of mine employs a black ceramic wall tile, which works well for her. Another possibility is a smooth black beach stone polished with oil.

To charge your black mirror with lunar virtue, set it so that it reflects the light of the full Moon and leave it for several hours. When not in use, keep it wrapped in black velvet or silk, or white linen. Both black and white are lunar colors.

HOW TO USE THE BLACK MIRROR

When using a black mirror for scrying, you usually do not wish to see a reflection in the mirror. Therefore, it is not necessary to tilt the mirror so that your eyes are perpendicular to its surface, as it would be if you sought to see your own face. You can leave the mirror lying flat upon the surface of the scrying table and look into it from an angle, just as you do when using the crystal or the water bowl. Imagine that its surface is liquid, and that you are looking through its surface into the depths of the mirror.

First the mirror will brighten to a gray. Colors will come and go across its surface in swift changes. You will probably see blue and purple and green, and even pink and violet. These colored clouds, which also appear in the depths of the crystal, have their own meanings, which have been interpreted psychically in connection with the human aura. Meaning may also be derived from the way the clouds are moving. You should not attach too much importance to these preliminary colors unless one color or motion is persistent in returning again and again.

INTERPRETING THE COLORS OF THE CLOUDS

The meanings of the colors given below are in part drawn from the classic work *Thought-Forms* by the Theosophists Annie Besant and C. W. Leadbeater, first published in 1901. I have also consulted *Crystal Gazing and Clairvoyance* by John Melville (London:

1896), which contains some interesting observations on the colors. The accuracy of these interpretations has been generally verified by my own work with the black mirror. However, you should realize that these colors are to some extent subjective, and will vary from scryer to scryer:

White—in general, good
    Pure white—truth, purity of purpose
    Brilliant white—spirituality, joy
    White shot with gold—revelation, prophecy
    Cream white—presence of angels
Yellow—in general, intellect
    Bright yellow—playfulness, mind games
    Pale yellow—abstract thought
    Yellow ochre—willfulness, mental dominance
    Golden yellow—creativity
Orange—in general, ambition
    Dark orange—pride
    Bright orange—achievement
    Pale orange—knowledge, teaching
    Dirty orange—selfishness
Red—in general, anger
    Scarlet-orange—indignation, righteous anger
    Vivid scarlet—fury, rage, violent impulse
    Very dark red—lust, perverse desire, brutality
    Dull crimson—sexual desire
    Bright crimson—emotional love, friendship
    Rose—spiritual love, devotion
Green—in general, desire
    Gray-green—deceitfulness
    Dark green flecked with scarlet—jealousy
    Spring green—flirting, teasing
    Emerald—sympathy, empathy

Blue—in general, devotion
    Deep blue—adoration
    Sky blue—self-sacrifice
    Pale slate—religious awe
    Blue-white—superstitious fear
    Violet-blue—idealism
Purple—in general, health
    Red-purple—animal vitality
    Dark purple—brooding, obsessive thoughts
    Pale purple—weakness, sickness
    Dirty brown-purple—insanity
    Blue-purple—perverse fantasies, erotic
        dreams
Brown—in general, materialism
    Bright brown—acquisitiveness
    Dull brown—miserliness, hoarding
    Rust—prideful possession, vanity
    Dark brown—envy, collecting mania
Gray—in general, sorrow
    Deep slate gray—depression
    Leaden gray—fear
    Putty gray—tedium, boredom
    Mist gray—emptiness
Black—in general, evil
    Glossy black—spite, vindictiveness, pettiness
    Dull black—brooding evil, murderous
        thoughts

INTERPRETING THE MOVEMENTS OF THE CLOUDS

These colors do not remain static, but billow and move across the depths of the mirror restlessly, one displacing the next almost before the first can form itself. The movements have traditional meanings in crystal scrying which also apply to the magic mirror. I have adapted these meanings slightly in my own work in a way that makes better sense to me.

For example, Melville says that things appearing on the left side are real, and things appearing on the right side are symbolic.[30] This is correct as far as it goes. The left side is the physical side, and the right is the intellectual side. Things on the left may be considered "real" in the sense that they pertain to matter. Things seen on the right may be considered "symbolic" in the sense that they are astral or mental. However, as every magician comes to understand, mental things are no less real than physical things.

> Clouds forming on the left—material matters, manifestations
> Clouds forming on the right—ideas, insights, spiritual matters
> Clouds moving left to right—approach of spirits, beginning
> Clouds moving right to left—withdrawal of spirits, ending
> Clouds rising—revelation, affirmation (yes)
> Clouds falling—concealment, negation (no)

WORKING WITH THE CLOUDS

What you see at the start of a scrying session may look very much like clouds, as it does for most scryers. Or it may appear to resemble rushing water, or flashing lights, or moving shadows. Whatever this common phenomenon resembles, you should have little difficulty achieving it if you fix your gaze strongly at the heart of the mirror and strive to look through the glass as though it were the pane of a window that opens upon a night scene soon to be illuminated by dawn.

If you formulate specific questions in your mind while watching the motion of these clouds, you can gain useful information from the mirror without ever actually reaching the stage of seeing visions. The color and motion of the clouds will change in response to your thoughts. This is a blessing for many scryers because it is often much more difficult to see detailed images and hear articulate voices than to see the moving colors and shadows.

SIX DEGREES OF MIRROR SCRYING

As I mentioned in Chapter Three, John Melville divides clairvoyants into six degrees of attainment, basing his table on the one given by Jacob Dixon in his book *Hygienic Clairvoyance*. We might well question Melville's percentages, but they do indicate the gulf that lies between someone with a slight flair for psychic matters and a genuine seer.

Accepting his six grades for the sake of argument, and applying them to mirror scrying, I would judge that anyone in the first degree can see the moving clouds in the black mirror, but only those of the fourth degree or higher will be able to achieve detailed visions of spirits or worldly events.

Those of the fourth degree will see detached visions only irregularly and will not be able to summon them at will. Those of the fifth degree will be able to call up detached visions whenever desired. Those of the sixth and highest degree will achieve fully involving visions that engage all the five senses and draw the scryer into them as an actor in the drama.

Detached visions are those scried images that appear within the mirror like still photographs or moving film images. They are separate and apart from the scryer, who is a mere observer of the events that unfold within the mirror. Involving visions engage the scryer directly. Spirits may look at the scryer, address the scryer in conversation, or touch the scryer. The visions may appear to exist outside the limits of the mirror and to surround the scryer on all sides.

According to Melville's numbers, almost two-thirds of the general population can achieve some psychic sensitivity with practice, but only fourteen percent can attain the fourth level (which I associate with intermittent detached visions). Only two percent can become full-fledged seers who approach the proficiency of a Nostradamus or an Edward Kelley.

ADVICE FOR BEGINNERS

I do not mean to discourage you with these numbers. However, it is a fact of life that not everyone who tries to draw will become a Picasso, not everyone who plays the piano will turn into a Glen Gould, and not everyone who scries will become another Nostradamus. You should approach the mirror with the practical intention of getting as much out of it as you can, by putting as much into it as you can. Hard work can often make up for a lack of innate talent, at least in part.

When you finally do begin to see images in the mirror, they will probably appear tiny and far away, just as they do at first within the crystal. Do not attempt to seize upon these visions and pull them toward you. This is the surest way to banish them. Instead, continue to look deeper into the depths of the mirror and allow the visions to approach of their own accord.

Do not attempt to interact with the figures you may see in your early scried visions. If some of these beings nod in your direction, wink, speak to you or make other contacts with you, either remain impassive or nod politely. It is not necessary for you to speak out loud. If you direct your thoughts at these spirits, they will hear you just as clearly as though you had spoken.

How Spirits "Hear" Thoughts

Spirits "hear" your thoughts before you articulate them in your own consciousness. Your verbal stream of consciousness is actually just an echo of the original fountain of your thoughts. By this I mean that first, a thought comes to you below the level of words, and second, you shape it into words and play it back in your own mind.

For example, you may have the wordless realization that you are hungry. A moment later you tell yourself "I'm getting hungry." The actual voiced thought is a response to an earlier thought that was not framed in the English language. Spirits are able to perceive and understand these unvoiced primary thoughts when these thoughts are directed at them. They cannot hear your own private thoughts if you take care not to direct these at the spirits. If you think something, then think to yourself "I mustn't let the spirits hear this thought," it is already too late. By directing your awareness at the spirits with the secret thought in mind, you have already communicated that thought to the spirits.

For this reason, I find the best policy with scried spirits is to be completely honest. Tell them everything, hide nothing. You cannot be tricked into betraying a secret if you refuse to have secrets. This approach has the added advantage that it tends to make the spirits more truthful and forthcoming. They automatically respond to your candor with revelations of their own.

THE GOLDEN RULE FOR SPIRITS

This is a general rule with spirits. Treat them with respect, they respond with respect. Treat them with love, they respond with love. Treat them truthfully, they respond with truth. On the other hand, if you try to dominate them they will attempt to dominate you. If you lie to them, they will lie to you. If you hurt them, they will try their level best to hurt you back. A scryer who is always respectful, decent, loving, and truthful is in very little danger from any spirit. At least, this has been my personal experience.

CHAPTER 16

Egyptian Lamp Scrying

ORIGINS OF FIRE SCRYING

Fire scrying extends back to before the time of
Zoroaster in Persia (seventh century B.C.), who merely rationalized a cult of fire that was ancient when he
was born. It was practiced in many diverse cultures
from Ireland to India. Atar, the Persian god of fire,
was the spiritual fire in the heavens as well as the
physical fire that dwells in burning wood. Bonfires
were lit in his honor, under various names, throughout Celtic Europe and the pagan nations of the Middle East in biblical times.

PASSING THROUGH THE FIRE

The custom of passing children through the fire of
Moloch was condemned by the writers of the Old Testament: "And they caused their sons and daughters
to pass through the fire, and used divination and
enchantments, and sold themselves to do evil in the
sight of the Lord, to provoke him to anger" (2 Kings
17:17). Passing through the fire did not involve the

sacrifice of infants, as is sometimes mistakenly believed, but was a form of fire walking or fire leaping.

The identical rite was still being practiced in Ireland in the eighteenth century, as this contemporary account testifies:

> Being at a gentleman's house about 30 miles West of Dublin, he told us, that on the 21st of June we should see an odd sight at midnight. Accordingly, at that hour, he conducted us out upon the top of his house, where, in a few minutes, to our great astonishment, we saw fires lighted on all the high places round, some nearer and some more distant. We had a pretty extensive view, and, I should suppose, might see about 15 miles each way. There were many heights in this extent; and on every height was a fire: I counted not less than 40. We amused ourselves with watching them, and with betting which hill would be lighted first. Not long after, on a more attentive view, I discovered shadows of people near the fire, and round it; and every now and then they quite darkened it. I enquired the reason of this, and what they were about; and was immediately told, they were not only dancing round, but passing through the fire; for, that it was the custom of the country, on that day, to make their families, their sons, and their daughters, and their cattle, pass through the fire; without which they could expect no success in their dairies, nor in the crops, that year.[31]

THE FEAST OF JOHN THE BAPTIST

That the power of fire was connected to the sense of vision in these rites honoring the god Baal (another form of Atar) is confirmed by the following passage

from a Latin work that was translated into English
for Queen Elizabeth I in 1570:

> Then doth the joyfull feast of John the Baptist take
>   his turne,
> When bonfires great, with lofty flame, in every towne
>   doe burne,
> And young men round about with maydes doe daunce
>   in every street
> With garlands wrought of motherwort, or else of ver-
>   vaine sweet,
> And many other flowers faire, with violets in their
>   hands;
> Where as they all doe fondly thinke that whosoever
>   stands
> And thorow the flowers beholds the flame, his eyes
>   shall feel no paine,
> When thus 'till night they daunced have, they through
>   the fire amain
> With striving minds doe run, and all their herbs they
>   cast therein;
> And then with words devout, and prayers, they
>   solemnly begin,
> Desiring God that all their illes may there confounded
>   be;
> Whereby they thinke through all that yeare from
>   augues to be free.[32]

The feast of the nativity of St. John the Baptist
took place on June 24. It was a form of summer solstice celebration, completely pagan in its origins, just
as Christmas is founded upon the pagan Yuletide observation of the winter solstice. The first observes the
longest day, while the second observes the shortest.

Quite naturally, both are closely connected with the worship of fire, the earthly light that mimics the glory of the Sun.

ST. JOHN'S PLANT

It is interesting from the perspective of practical magic that specific herbs were offered to the flames, and that to look at the Baal fire through a garland of one of these herbs was thought to strengthen the faculty of sight and protect the eyes from any disease or weakness throughout the remainder of the year. It would be natural to extend this occult virtue one step further, and associate the light of the fire seen through the ring of flowering herbs with second sight.

The motherwort referred to is mugwort or St. John's plant *(Artemisia vulgaris)*. It was fabled that John the Baptist had worn a girdle made from this herb while dwelling in the wilderness. Garlands of it collected and worn about the head on St. John's Eve were believed to guard the wearer against misfortunes and possession by evil spirits.

FIRE SCRYING VERSUS FIRE DIVINATION

Fire scrying is probably as old as fire worship. It began when Stone Age humans first learned to tend and preserve a flame upon their hearths. It is important not to confuse fire scrying with fire divination. Fire scrying is the art of obtaining extrasensory information by the agents of the unconscious mind in the form of sensory metaphors. Fire divination is the interpretation of various motions and shapes of flame and its related phenomena according to a set system of rules.

When we do fire scrying, we see images in the fire. When we do fire divination, we see only the flame, and interpret its meaning by how it moves and shapes itself. No second sight or psychic ability is needed for fire divination beyond an ability to recognize and correctly interpret the omens of the flames.

For example, the country folk in Lincolnshire, England, believed that they could foretell death by the shape of a candle flame. If the flame twisted round and round as it rose from the wick, this was known as the "winding sheet," and foreshadowed the imminent death of someone nearby. Another death omen by fire was the "coffin," an ember in the form of a burial casket that exploded with a crack and a sheet of sparks to land on the outer edge of the hearth.

We are not directly concerned with flame omens, except when they indicate the presence of a spirit or angel during the scrying. When an angel appears within the flame of the candle or lamp, the flame is nourished by this presence and becomes very tall and still, sometimes extending as much as three or four times beyond its natural height. When a spirit of a mixed or low nature is present in the flame, it begins to spark and dance around, and to flutter with an audible sound for no apparent reason.

EGYPTIAN LAMP SCRYING

The Babylonians and Egyptians practiced scrying by means of the flame of an oil lamp. The lamp itself was of stone, a low open dish with a strip of white linen coiled in the oil that had its end draped over the edge of the dish. Sometimes the dish has an elongated ledge or channel for the end of the linen wick to lie upon. The extended end of the wick was lighted. The oil rose up the wick by capillary action and nourished the flame. As the wick burned down, more of its length was pulled out of the oil and draped over the edge of the lamp.

The Egyptians used "clear Oasis oil," which was probably a kind of palm oil. You may use any vegetable oil, the clearer and purer the better. A good quality olive oil is fine. Either fashion your lamp from artist's clay or use a small ceramic or stone dish that has a broad rim—a small ashtray will work well. Make sure it is a new ashtray. Do not use a vessel that has been soiled in the past, no matter how well you clean it.

The Egyptians say nothing about the lamp except that it must not be red in color. Red was the color of the god Set, the god of evil who is equivalent to Satan in the Egyptian pantheon. Do not use a red lamp unless you wish to communicate with the infernal demons. White ceramic will make an excellent scrying lamp.

BRICKS OR TILES FOR ELEVATION

Set your oil lamp upon your scrying table and sit on the west side facing east across the lamp. Both you and the lamp should be elevated from the floor upon new bricks. I suggest that you buy a box of unglazed ceramic floor tiles, each tile about 4 by 4 inches in size and of some natural Earth color such as gray or brown or black—but not red. Or you can use actual bricks, as the Egyptians did, but avoid bright red bricks. Place a tile beneath each of the legs of your scrying chair, and each leg of your scrying table.

This is more of a symbolic than a practical measure. You will likely be living in a wooden house with an elevated wooden floor. The Egyptians lived at ground level, and their floors mostly consisted of packed mud or paving stones. When they elevated themselves upon new bricks, it was to break the direct contact between the scryer and the Earth.

If you place tiles or bricks under your table and chair, be sure to also elevate your feet. These tiles will symbolically raise you and the lamp toward heaven, separating you from the dampening influence of the Earth.

PAINTING THE EYES

It was common for Egyptian scryers to paint their eyes with magically potent colors and herbal substances intended to encourage second sight. Green and blue colors are appropriate. This eye makeup should be very bold. You may wish to draw upon your eyes the image of the utchat, the famous symbol of the eye so common in Egyptian art. The utchat of Thoth, which consisted of the eye symbol with a broad upturned lunar crescent beneath it, is appropriate. Paint this upon your left eye, which is your lunar and receptive side.

You may also wish to paint the utchat of Ra upon your right eye. This is the same familiar Egyptian eye symbol, but without the lunar crescent beneath it. These symbols were called the white eye (right) and the black eye (left) of Horus, respectively the Sun and the Moon.

To make this makeup magically active, it is best to mix it with a little juice of mugwort, vervain or other scrying herbs. It is not really necessary to draw an elaborate design around your eyes, but the act of painting the lids can become a standard part of your scrying ritual, and can be very effective in keying in the necessary receptive mental state for scrying.

Women may be more inclined to use this eye painting technique than men, who, if they prefer, can merely wipe a little of the juice of mugwort or some other visionary herb over their eyelids. This can be obtained simply by crushing a leaf of the herb between the thumb and fingers. This juice should also be smeared on the forehead between the eyebrows, at the location of the third eye.

Collyries Not Recommended

In ancient times it was the custom of scryers to put herbal salves directly into the eyes themselves. These concoctions, called collyries, were compounded of many rare or noxious substances. For example in the medieval grimoire of natural magic titled *The Marvels of the World,* the following recipe is given: "If thou wilt see that other men can not. Take the gall of a male Cat, and the fat of a Hen all white, and mix them together, and anoint thy eyes, and thou shalt see it that others can not see."[33] These occult eye salves were probably injurious to the sight, and cannot be recommended here for use in modern scrying.

The Method for Lamp Scrying

The instructions given in the Egyptian grimoires say to stare directly at the flame of the lamp without looking away and without becoming afraid. Eventually, if you have success, you will see light shining out of the flame of the lamp. This is a spiritual radiance, which is much brighter than the color of the material fire.

You can address your invocation to the Greco-Roman god who rules the day upon which you perform the lamp scrying. These gods and goddesses are more familiar than the obscure Egyptian and Gnostic deities mentioned in the magical papyri. They are:

Day	Greek	Roman
Sunday	Helios	Sol
Monday	Selene	Luna
Tuesday	Ares	Mars
Wednesday	Hermes	Mercury
Thursday	Zeus	Jupiter
Friday	Aphrodite	Venus
Saturday	Cronus	Saturn

Chant the following invocation so that your breath strikes the flame of the lamp and causes it to flutter gently. If the air is still in the scrying chamber, as it should be, it will not take much breath to stir the flame. Insert the name of the god or goddess of the day upon which you perform the lamp scrying in the two spaces.

INVOCATION TO THE GOD OF THE DAY

O great _____, thou who art amongst the seven lights in the crown of the Supreme God who gives light abundantly, the companion of the flame, in whose mouth is the flame which is not quenched, the great God that dieth not, the great God that sitteth in the flame, who is in the lake of heaven, in whose hand is

the greatness and might of the God, come within in the
midst of this flame and reveal thyself today; inquire for
me concerning everything about which I shall ask here
today; for I will glorify thee in heaven before the stars,
I will glorify thee on the Earth, I will glorify thee
before Him who sitteth upon the throne, who perisheth
not, He of the great glory, in whose hand is the greatness and might of God, he of the great glory, Elohim
Sabaoth, O great great God, who is above heaven, in
whose hand is the beautiful staff, who created the
gods, the gods not having created Him, come in to me
with _____, do thou give strength to my eyes,
cause me to see thee, cause my ears to hear thee when
thou speakest; and do thou inquire for me concerning
everything and every word I shall ask you here today.

This invocation should be chanted softly up to
seven times. It is not necessary to memorize the exact
wording, provided your intention is clear. You are
summoning the god of the day by the authority of
the Supreme God of heaven to act as your spiritual
guide and aid in the transmission of visions. You do
honor to the god of the day in your hymn, but even
greater honor to the Supreme God who rules over all
the days.

It is not necessary to name the Supreme God,
although you may use the name of your personal con-
ception of the highest deity if you wish. The name
that is used in the Egyptian ritual is "Sabaoth," a
Hebrew word meaning the angelic host of heaven,
specifically the angels who stand around the throne
of God. It is especially applied to the Sun, Moon, and
planets, making it very appropriate for our purposes.
Sabaoth was probably used by the Egyptian magician

who wrote the ritual simply as a barbarous name of power. You may wish to employ the more intelligible form Elohim Sabaoth, which translates God of Hosts.

The Formula of Light

If the god of the day is slow to manifest his or her presence, speak the following magic formula into the flame of the lamp so that it flutters:

> Grow, O light, come forth O light, rise O light, lift thyself up O light, come forth O light of God, reveal thyself to me, O servant of God, in whose hand is the command of today, who will inquire for me.

Moving Shadows

With your eyes continuing to focus upon the flame of the lamp, you will begin to see moving shadows off to the sides. These will vanish if you look directly at them, so continue to fix your gaze upon the lamp, but watch the shadows and moving shapes at the sides of your vision. This takes a little practice. The natural impulse is to shift your gaze to where you direct your awareness. You must learn to divide your point of awareness from your point of vision. It is quite possible to hold your eyes upon one place, yet watch something to the side of your field of view by moving only your attention, not your eyes.

When the shifting shadows or other shapes indicate the presence of the god of the day, mentally or verbally direct this god by name to present the information you desire either by speech or vision. Which form the god uses will depend on your scrying ability.

If you can see visions easily, the god is more likely to present the information you seek in a still image or moving drama. If you find it very easy to hear spirit voices, the god may give you most of what you seek through speech.

OTHER SIGNS FROM THE GOD OF THE DAY

If, as often happens, your scrying abilities are more limited, you must remain attentive and look for any signs that the god of the day may use to communicate with you. These will be given in response to simple yes-no questions, and may come in the form of a touch upon your face, the sensation of a breeze upon your skin, a stirring within your body, a bright flash of light, a movement at the edge of your vision, a musical tone inside your head, or (quite commonly) that old standby of spiritualists, a sharp rap upon the table, floor, door, or some other part of the house.

If you plan to work often with the seven planetary gods, you should read up on them and learn as much about their qualities and abilities as you are able. Fortunately, a great deal has been written concerning these gods and goddesses. Any good book on Greek mythology will provide you with what you need. Especially important is to have a clear mental image of the appearance of each god when you invoke that god into the flame.

CANDLE SCRYING VERSUS LAMP SCRYING

The lamp scrying described above can easily be done with a candle. You may find it less trouble to use candles rather than attending to the wick of the lamp, which must be frequently adjusted and repositioned as it burns down. If you use a lamp, experiment with adding scented oils to the oil of the lamp. It can be useful to associate a different scent for each of the seven days, if you can find seven that you like. If not, it is better to use only one scent, or no scent at all. When performing fire scrying with a candle flame, you can employ scented candles, or simply burn incense at the side of the table upon your incense burner.

FIRE GAZING

There is another form of fire scrying that was often practiced by country folk in Europe. For this you need a fireplace. Build a large fire of hardwood logs, and when it has burned down to a bed of brightly glowing embers, sit in silence before the fire and regard the changing colors and varying brightness that moves across the surface of the embers. After a while you will begin to see pictures in the embers, and the crackling sparks may begin to talk to you. This is an excellent scrying method for long winter nights.

You can also do this form of fire scrying out-of-doors seated before a campfire or ceremonial bonfire. In Germany and Scandinavia bonfires are still made on New Year's Eve, a survival of the ancient pagan custom. Participants write down their wishes for the coming year on slips of paper, and exactly at midnight they cast these into the flames. I participated in such a ceremony with a small group of associates and found it to be an evocative and potent experience. It is a good occasion for scrying the embers, provided the night is not too cold and windy.

CHAPTER 17

The Pendulum

ROMAN PENDULUM SCRYING

The pendulum was used for scrying by the ancient Romans. We are fortunate enough to have a detailed description of the method preserved in the writings of the Roman historian Ammianus Marcellinus, who recorded the proceedings of a conspiracy trial against a group who plotted the assassination of the Emperor of the East, Valens (reigned 364-378).

During the course of the trial, inquiry was made about a curious little table found in the possession of the plotters. One of the men, who was named Hillarius, confessed under torture that they had used the table magically when trying to predict who would succeed Valens to the throne:

> Honored judges, we constructed this unfortunate little table that you see here after the fashion of the tripod at Delphi, with dark incantations, out of branches of laurel; and with imprecations of secret song, and numerous ceremonies repeated over daily, we consecrated it by magic rites, till at last we put it in motion.

When it reached this capacity of movement, as often as we wished to interrogate it by secret inquiry, we proceeded thus.

It was placed in the middle of a room purified throughout by Arabian perfumes; a round dish was simply laid upon it, formed of a composite material of many metals. On the phlange of its outer round were skillfully engraved the scriptile forms of the alphabet separated into as many exactly measured spaces. Over this basin a man stood clothed in linen garments and shod with linen socks, his head bound round with a turban-like tuft of hair, and bearing a rod of vervain, the prospering plant. After we had favorably conciliated the deity, who is the giver of all presage, with duly formulated charms and ceremonial knowledge, he communicated a gentle movement to a ring that hung suspended over the basin.... This was tied up by an exceedingly fine Carpathian thread, which had been initiated with mystical observances. This ring, moving by little leaps or jumps, so as to alight upon the distinct intervals with the separate letters inscribed, each in its compartment to itself, gives out in heroic verse answers suitable to the inquiries made, comprehended perfectly in number and measure; such as are called Pythic, or those delivered by the oracles of the Branchidae.[34]

DID NOSTRADAMUS USE A PENDULUM?

As I said in the chapter on Nostradamus, it is just barely possible that the French seer used this Roman method of basin scrying by means of a pendulum to produce individual letters that formed intelligible prophetic verses. This would explain how the god who was "seated near" (his personal daemon or guardian angel), could speak to him. The "voice" he mentions in the quatrain titled "The Magical Call By Water" would in this case be the bell-like sound of the ring striking the inner sides of the metal basin.

THE ROMAN METHOD

When Hillarius says that the bowl was "a composite material of many metals," he means that it was made of electrum, an alloy of gold and silver that occurred naturally, and was composed of about one-fifth silver to four-fifths gold. It was also blended artificially, where the silver content ranged from one-quarter to one-half of the alloy. Medieval alchemists also employed the name for an alloy of the seven planetary metals (gold, silver, tin, copper, iron, lead, and mercury). Electrum was favored for magical purposes by those who could afford it. Being composed of all seven planetary metals, it attracted the rays of all seven planets and stored up their occult virtues.

When he speaks of "vervain, the prospering plant" he simply means that the shoot of vervain was living and had green leaves upon it. The movement that was communicated to the ring that hung within the basin upon its "Carpathian" thread was probably imparted by the vervain wand. Presumably the thread was attached to the end of the wand. In order to operate this scrying instrument, a very long thread would be needed so that the ring would swing quite freely within the rim of the basin, and continue to rebound from the sides once an initial momentum had been imparted to it.

The ring itself, which is not described, was probably a simple band of electrum with occult characters engraved upon it. These may have included the name of the "deity, who is the giver of all presage"— presumably Apollo, whose oracles were famous throughout the ancient world. It would need to be fairly heavy in order to rebound effectively from the sides of the basin.

The twenty-four letters of the Greek alphabet were engraved into the flange of the basin. Presumably this flange was a broad, flat rim extending out from the sides of the basin. The sides would have risen almost vertically, or even curved inward a bit, to afford a flat striking surface for the ring—a shallow dish would not work very well. Hillarius says nothing about water in the basin, but water would act as an effective reservoir for storing lunar virtue. Nostradamus certainly did use water, but whether he employed a ring suspended on a thread from a wand of vervain is less clear.

Regarding the scrying table itself, Hillarius obviously considered this important. He speaks of "dark incantations" and "imprecations of secret song, and numerous ceremonies repeated over daily" with which the conspirators consecrated the table. It was a table of three legs made out of branches of laurel, and may not have had a top as such, but may have been merely a tripod upon which to support the scrying basin. You will recall that laurel, or sweetwood, was the substance specified by the Enochian angels for the scrying table of John Dee.

The "turban-like tuft of hair" around the head of the man in linen is puzzling. Presumably this was a braid or narrow strip of animal hair or fur wound around the head several times, probably three times. I can only guess at its composition. It may have been a braided rope of horse's hair. The horse was connected with divination and oracles by the Germans, who made up a significant portion of the population of Rome in the fourth century, having gradually acquired citizenship through service in the Roman legions. There is a small but distinctly unpleasant possibility that it was a braided rope of human hair cut from a corpse. The Romans associated scrying with the dead and often employed necromantic rites.

USE OF THE PENDULUM IS SCRYING, NOT DIVINATION

The reason this pendulum method qualifies as scrying and not divination is because the thread on which the ring hung suspended was supported upon a wand of vervain in the hand of a man. This allowed the deep mind of the man dressed in linen to communicate information through the basin by means of subliminal muscular contractions that moved the ring in non-random ways. Had the ring been suspended from the ceiling and allowed to blow in the breeze from a window, it would have been a divination. Since the method involved the communication of data from the unconscious mind to the conscious awareness through the avenues of the senses, it was a scrying, as the term is used in this book.

This method of the pendulum in a basin inscribed with letters of the alphabet is essentially the same as the Ouija board method we use today. Small involuntary movements in the arm and hand holding the thread are used to spell out answers to specific questions. There are two other methods for using the pendulum that are still employed in modern times. These are simplifications of the ancient Roman method.

THE RING AND GLASS METHOD

The older of the two, which has been used for centuries in Europe, involves the suspension of a ring from a thin silk thread inside an ordinary water goblet or glass tumbler. The scryer sits at a table with the elbow of the scrying hand resting on the surface of the table and holds the thread between the fingers of the scrying hand (I recommend the left hand, which is more receptive to unconscious influences in those who are right-handed). The ring that serves as the bob of the pendulum is allowed to hang inside the glass very close to the side—no more than a quarter of an inch between the ring and the glass.

Responses from this oracle come in the form of tapping sounds as the ring gently raps the side of the glass. The scryer asks a specific question that can be answered by yes or no, then waits for the response. A single tap against the glass is usually understood to indicate yes, while two taps close together indicate no. A series of rapid taps is given when the oracle is uncertain of the correct response.

THE RING AND CROSS METHOD

The other modern pendulum method uses the same physical posture for the scryer and the same ring and thread, but in place of the glass tumbler, a sheet of paper is laid on the surface of the table with a large cross marked upon it. The ring is held suspended over the intersection of the cross in the left hand upon its silk thread. As in the previous method, a simple question is asked that requires only a yes or a no answer.

The ring of the pendulum soon begins to trace a small circle around the intersection of the cross, moving either clockwise or counterclockwise. When the answer is yes, it begins to swing back and forth along the vertical arm of the cross. When the answer is no, it swings from side to side along the horizontal arm of the cross.

There is another interpretation of this method. Some users of the pendulum read a circular motion of the ring in a clockwise direction as a yes, and an opposite circular motion in a counterclockwise direction as a no. It does not matter which way of reading the motions of the ring you choose, provided that you are perfectly clear about it in your own mind before you begin.

You should try this simple method of divination, which requires nothing more than a ring, a thread, and a sheet of paper. It is amazingly easy to produce the up-and-down and side-to-side swinging of the ring, which occurs in a completely involuntary way. However, it is more difficult to get reliable, consistent responses from this oracle. To use it effectively, you must practice with the pendulum regularly and observe all the aspects of cleansing, prayer, and ritual preparations described earlier in this book.

ROCK CRYSTAL PENDULUMS

Many modern scryers prefer to use a small natural rock crystal in place of a ring. You should be able to buy a crystal the size of the last two joints of your baby finger that is of good quality for under ten dollars. Crystals are vastly overpriced in many occult bookstores. Remember when buying that quality is the key factor. A crystal that is full of cracks, cloudiness, and occlusions (small bits of sand trapped within the crystal) is almost worthless, despite what the store owner may try to charge you for it. For use as a pendulum you do not want a large, heavy crystal. One that is about the same weight as a penny works well.

Most rock crystals have a good end that shows the natural taper of the crystal, and a bad end where the crystal has been banged out of its rock matrix by some rock hound with a hammer. You should attach a small copper, brass, or silver loop (silver is best) of wire to the jagged end by means of a drop of glue. Epoxy works well. So does the clear liquid so-called super glue. When dry, tie a piece of fine thread to this loop and trim off the excess. Silk thread is recommended, but you can use a synthetic thread if you cannot get real silk. A fine silver chain will also yield good results.

PURIFYING THE PENDULUM

Once you have made your pendulum, you should purify it. Purification removes all the occult associations or impressions the crystal and thread may have picked up during their travels. A simple way to accomplish this is to fill a clear bowl with fresh, pure water. Holding the pendulum by its thread over the bowl, pronounce the cleansing prayer upon it just as though it were a living person. As you do so, place your own awareness within the crystal momentarily by means of the point visualization you learned earlier. You do this by mentally projecting the three perpendicular lines of intersection through the heart of the crystal, and imagining your point of self-awareness inside the crystal where the lines meet:

> Purge me with hyssop, and I shall be clean,
> Wash me, and I shall be whiter than snow,
> Create in me a clean heart, O God,
> And renew a right spirit within me.

Wiccans and pagans will undoubtedly prefer to use the cleansing prayer of the Goddess given in Chapter Four. Or if neither prayer suits you, compose your own prayer of cleansing that fulfills your specific purposes and is in perfect harmony with your beliefs. The prayers you compose yourself are always the most powerful.

Solemnly dip the crystal and its thread beneath the surface of the water in the bowl and allow them to lie in the water for several minutes. Visualize all the lingering contamination and acquired influences flowing out from the crystal and thread into the surrounding water, which you should visualize as darkening slightly. Remove the pendulum by its thread and visualize it as shining with white light. Place it upon a perfectly clean paper towel or cloth. Pour the astrally darkened water down the sink drain.

LUNAR CHARGING

Once the crystal has been purified, it may be charged with lunar virtue. On the night of the full Moon, set the pendulum and thread where the moonlight will fall directly upon it for several hours. The light of the

Moon is most potent when the Moon is high in the heavens, so you should do this around midnight. You can increase the effectiveness of this charging process. Put the crystal and its thread into a bowl of clean water with a small pinch of salt added and set the bowl under the rays of the full Moon. The salt water concentrates and stores lunar virtue.

You may find that the pendulum is more responsive if you place a small dish of water that has been charged with lunar virtue beneath the paper with the cross. Or if you are using the glass tumbler method, fill the glass halfway to the top with charged water and allow the pendulum to hang over it as it taps the inside rim of the glass.

A WATER PENDULUM

A variation on this approach is to make the pendulum itself out of charged water. If you can find a very tiny glass bottle (by tiny, I mean no larger than the end of your baby finger), you can fill this with water and charge it with moonlight. This bottle must be extremely small and light or it will not swing freely. The more magical the source of your water, the more potent it will be in use. If possible, try to draw it from a sacred well, pool, spring, river, or lake that has a long history of magic happenings.

Be certain that the bottle hangs straight down on its thread. If you merely tie the thread around the neck of the bottle, it will hang crooked and not work properly. You must glue a ring onto the center of the cap, or onto the center of the underside of the bottle, and tie your thread to this support.

One way to make a very small vessel for charged water is to get a length of glass tubing about a quarter of an inch in diameter, carefully break off an inch or so, and plug one end with a thick blob of epoxy glue. When this has set, fill the tube with sacred water and seal the water into the tube by plugging the other end with another blob of glue. Attach a metal ring to this second blob of glue before it sets so that you will have a place to tie your thread.

DESTRUCTIVE EFFECTS OF SUNLIGHT

Never allow the scrying pendulum or any other tool associated with it to lie exposed to direct sunlight. The Sun will neutralize the occult virtue of the Moon that is in your crystal pendant naturally, and will expel any additional charge of lunar virtue you may have infused into it by exposing it to moonlight. Immediately after use, always wrap up your scrying instruments in white linen or black silk (dark blue may also be used), and store them away in a safe place out of the rays of the Sun.

CHAPTER 18

The Ouija Board

OUIJA DESCENDED FROM THE ROMAN PENDULUM

The earliest form of Ouija board appears to have been the ring and basin pendulum scrying method employed by the conspirators against the Roman Emperor Valens in the fourth century. This was undoubtedly used by the Greeks before the time of Christ, and was probably invented by them.

Nandor Fodor in his *Encyclopaedia of Psychic Science* quotes a French biography of Pythagoras that says the Pythagoreans held seances in which "a mystic table, moving on wheels, moved towards signs, which the philosopher and his pupil, Philolaus, interpreted to the audience as being revelations supposedly from the unseen world."[35] Unfortunately, Fodor does not bother to give the title or author of this French work. I have not been able to find any reference to symbol scrying by a moving table in the ancient biographies and references to Pythagoras.

ORIGIN OF THE OUIJA

The modern Ouija board appears to be the amalgamation of two separate instruments for scrying. The first is a wheel of the letters of the alphabet, which was laid out on small slips of paper on a smooth table. Into the middle of this was placed an inverted wine glass. Those seeking to scry by the glass placed their index fingers upon the base and asked their questions. The glass slid, apparently of its own volition, to spell out an answer on the letter wheel. This amusement was in vogue during the nineteenth century, and perhaps earlier. It is a simple adaptation of the pendulum method of the Romans, where a wine glass takes the place of the suspended ring.

The second part of the modern Ouija board is the planchette, a triangular or heart-shaped board a little smaller than the human hand, which is elevated an inch or so on three legs. This was invented in 1853 by a French spiritist (the French term for "spiritualist") named Planchette as an aid to automatic writing. It had small rollers at the ends of its two rear legs and a hole in the tip to accommodate a pencil, which formed the single front leg. When a sheet of paper was placed under the planchette, automatic movements by the hand of the operator caused the pencil to write on the paper.

THE OUIJA BOARD IN AMERICA

In 1891 a patent was granted to Elijah J. Bond on the first modern Ouija board. This was purchased the following year by William Fuld, who started to manufacture his "Oriole Talking Boards" at the Southern Novelty Company of Baltimore, later to be renamed the Baltimore Talking Board Company. The name *Ouija* literally means yes-yes (French *oui;* German *ja).* I do not know when the word originated, but the *Oxford English Dictionary* gives 1904 as the first citation of its use, so presumably it is coequal, or nearly so, with the board itself.

In 1966 Parker Brothers bought the rights to the Ouija board and moved its manufacturing facilities from Baltimore to Salem, Massachusetts (who says businessmen have no sense of humor?). The board outsold that perennial Parker Brothers favorite, Monopoly, in the first full year at Salem. Over two million copies were shipped. This was at the dawn of the Hippie revolution when all things occult were the sudden rage.

CONSTRUCTION OF THE BOARD

Parker Brothers put out a good product, at least in the early days. I grew up using it. The board itself was made of heavy pressboard with a highly polished face. The planchette and its three removable legs were of solid hardwood. Small felt pads took the place of M. Planchette's little rollers. These allowed the planchette to slide like a cube of ice across the board.

Most persons are familiar with the layout of the modern board. However, if you have not seen one, I should explain that the English alphabet is arranged in two crescents, one above the other, that extend across the upper middle section of the board. In the upper left corner is the word *yes* beside a picture of the Sun. In the upper right corner is the word *no* beside a picture of the Moon. The numbers from one to nine are written in a straight line across the lower middle section of the board beneath the alphabet. At the very bottom are the words *good bye*.

HOW TO WORK THE OUIJA

The operation of the board is quite simple. At least two scryers sit facing each other with their knees nearly touching. The board is placed upon their knees. The planchette is set upon the middle of the board with its point directed toward the alphabet. Both scryers place the fingertips of both hands gently upon the planchette and move it around in small circles for a minute to loosen up their arms.

One of the scryers asks a simple question. It is usual to begin with questions that can be answered by a simple yes or no. The most common first question: "Is anybody there?" Surprisingly, this inane query often gets a response. After a few minutes the planchette begins to move with greater ease, and to spell out answers to more complex questions.

THE MOTION OF THE PLANCHETTE

The sensation of using the Ouija board is quite startling the first time. When the planchette begins to move, each scryer looks suspiciously at the others and asks whether they are deliberately moving it. Each denies any fraud. Even though everyone touching the planchette is absolutely certain that he or she is not moving the pointer, it slides across the surface of the board quickly and vigorously. Undoubtedly the motion is imparted by one of the scryers, perhaps more than one, but it is impossible to judge which is the automatic agent who is driving the planchette.

It is fairly easy to spot trickery. The planchette will slow and stop as though deliberately held down by a heavy hand, and then will move with slow jerks to spell out its message. This occurs when one of the scryers forces the pointer against its natural motions to give out a false message. When the planchette is allowed to move by itself, it slides effortlessly and smoothly in rapid darts and small circles, and seems to pull the hands of the scryers along with it.

One person alone can use the Ouija board, but he or she must be an accomplished scryer or must possess a strong natural gift for scrying to achieve success. It is much easier for two persons to operate the pointer. The famous English scryer Hester Travers Smith believed that two operators gave the best results. In her opinion, three created confusion in the responses.[36] When there are two operators, doubtlessly one is dominant and the other passive, although it is impossible to tell which is which during the scrying session.

PERILS OF THE "DEVIL BOARD"

Do not believe all the hysterical nonsense that has been written about the dangers of using the Ouija board. It is no more dangerous than any other medium of scrying. I have often read and heard it said that it is tempting fate to use the Ouija when alone. Nonsense! When scrying, you either get results or you do not. Whether you are alone or in company at the time is beside the point. There are no special perils attached to the Ouija. Why should there be? Indeed, I consider the Ouija board to be a safer scrying instrument than the crystal or black mirror.

If you are afraid of spirits, you probably should not be scrying in the first place. When scrying, the difficulty is not molestation by spirits. The hard part is getting the spirits to notice you at all. After scrying without success for several weeks, you might welcome the signs that some spirit is finally taking an interest in your existence.

ALL SCRYING INVOLVES LIMITED MEDIUMSHIP

All forms of automatism, active or passive, are limited forms of mediumship. In order to cause you to perceive impressions in the crystal, or work your muscles below the level of your conscious awareness to move the planchette, the agents of your deep mind must take partial control of your body. Every time you scry you are in this sense acting as a spirit host or medium.

Almost always this mediumship is limited in duration, location, and expression. Almost always it is completely voluntary on your part, and can be terminated by your conscious will whenever you choose. The observance of a regular time and place for scrying, and the use of a ritual framework, help to ensure that you retain total control. By linking the partial mediumship with a specific time, place, and set of ritual actions, you discourage it from occurring under other conditions.

METHOD OF SCRYING WITH THE OUIJA

When using the Ouija, it is a good idea to prepare a list of questions before you begin. This way, you will not find yourself staring into space and wondering what to ask the board. If the board is responsive, you are free to ask as many spontaneous follow-up questions as you wish to clarify any particular matter of inquiry before returning to your list. It is very helpful if a third person not working the planchette writes down all the questions and the responses of the pointer. Words can be difficult to pick out from the unbroken string of letters you will receive from the planchette unless they are recorded the instant they are received.

The scryer sitting at the base of the board, who can read the letters and numbers most easily, should call out the letters one after another as they are indicated by the planchette. If you are working alone, I suggest that you turn on a tape recorder at the beginning of the session and call out the letters into the machine. You can play the tape over after you have finished and sort out any words you may have missed.

Some sort of recorder, human or mechanical, is a necessity when the planchette is moving at top speed. Mrs. Smith writes: "The words come through so quickly that it is almost impossible to read them, and it requires an experienced shorthand writer to take them down when the traveller [i.e., the planchette] moves at its maximum speed."[37]

MAKING YOUR OWN OUIJA BOARD

If you do not own a Ouija board and cannot find one to buy, you can make your own in the traditional way by writing the letters of the alphabet on small squares of paper and taping them down firmly in a circle about eighteen inches in diameter. Choose a smooth surface such as a coffee table or dining table, and make sure that all the operators can reach the pointer easily no matter where in the circle it may move. The pointer can be a small, upturned wine goblet. You and your friends will probably only be able to fit a finger each on the base of the glass, but this is sufficient to activate it.

As an alternative, the alphabet may be written around the perimeter of a square on a large sheet of paper or smooth cardboard, the first seven letters across the top, the next six down the right side, the next seven across the bottom of the square, and the final six up the left side. You may want to write *yes* on the left and *no* on the right in the middle of this square to speed up the responses, and below them the numbers from one to nine. It is not really necessary to write *good bye* since, when the spirits of the board have said all they wish to say, they will cause the pointer to slide completely off or simply cease moving it.

DOES THE OUIJA BOARD EVER LIE?

The quality of responses you receive from the Ouija depends on your attitude while using it. Those who scry with the board as a party amusement and ask it silly questions are very likely to receive contemptuous and nonsensical responses. The spirits of the board toy with dabblers and fools. If you approach it with a serious and reverent attitude and seek answers to important questions, the board will respond in a serious way.

The responses you receive will not always be accurate in a physical sense, but they will be intended as accurate by the spirits, who often have difficulty understanding what is meant by simple physical truth—what we call fact. The truth familiar to spirits is the kind of truth you encounter during dreams. It is a spiritual truth, and does not always correspond to physical fact as we incarnates know it. The truth conveyed by the spirits of the board must be interpreted mythically and symbolically from a subjective point of view.

I use the term "spirits of the board" in exactly the same way the ancient Babylonians used the term "spirits of the thumb." The intelligences that respond to your questions by moving the planchette appear to be independent beings with their own thoughts and emotions, likes and dislikes, abilities and limitations. They may very well be expressions of your own unconscious mind, but this does not prevent them from being spirits.

No one really knows what spirits are, not even after thousands of years of communication with these beings. No one knows what the unconscious mind is, either, or where its boundaries lie, or the nature of its inhabitants. All that can be said is that the Ouija board responds as though the planchette is being moved by the invisible hand of a spirit, or several spirits in succession. You are free to call this motivating force any name you like. I call it a spirit.

CHAPTER 19

Aura Scrying

HALO, NIMBUS, AUREOLE, AND GLORY

Belief in the aura is ancient and universal. We are most familiar with it in Christian religious art, where it is represented as a radiance that surrounds the head, hands, or entire body of Jesus, the angels, and the saints. Medieval mystics and philosophers regarded the aura as an occasional expression in the servants of God of the unbearably brilliant and unfailing light that emanates from the godhead. When a saint achieved an extraordinary level of holiness through some act of sacrifice or internal devotion, the divine light of spirit broke through its prison of flesh and became visible to other human beings.

Four kinds of aura are recognized by the Church. In modern English references the nimbus is a cloud of light surrounding the head. The halo, which is usually stylized into a circle of light that floats above the crown of the head, but more properly should surround the head, was brighter and more concentrated. The aureole is a light that surrounds the body. The glory is the combined radiance of the aureole and the nimbus—what we more commonly consider to be the aura today.

In medieval times an aureole was defined as the light around the head, and a nimbus was the light around the body, but these terms were inverted by the French archaeologist Adolphe Napoleon Didron in his work *Histoire de Dieu* (1843). Later English reference works copied this error. Didron's mistake was not followed by French Church authorities, so confusion of these terms is inevitable.

The glory is sometimes depicted in religious art as the vesica or vesica piscis, a lens-shaped figure formed by the overlap of two equal circles that pass through each other at their centers. Christ, the Virgin Mary, and other saints are often painted within this pointed oval, which is also called a mandorla (from the Italian word for "almond").

THE SHINING FACE OF GOD

In addition to the light said to surround the saints, light was also observed to shine forth from their faces and stream out from their eyes, ears, nose, and mouth. When Moses came down from Mount Sinai with the tablets of the Ten Commandments, his face shone so brightly that the Hebrews were too terrified to approach him until he covered his face with a veil (Exodus 34:29-33). When Jesus was transfigured upon the mountain, "his face did shine as the sun, and his raiment was white as the light" (Matthew 17:2). It is reported of St. Philip of Neri that when his hand touched the chalice during the mass, his face glowed with mysterious light and sparks of fire flew from his eyes.

Such reports are not confined to Christianity. The Theosophist Madam Blavatsky mentions a Hindu religious painting of the goddess Devaki nursing Krishna, in which both the virgin goddess and the god are surrounded by aureoles. She further states that the aureole was used by the artists of Babylonia "whenever they desired to honor or deify a mortal's head."[38]

OCCULT CONCEPTS OF THE AURA

The German Renaissance magician Paracelsus (1490-1541) makes mention of the aura, saying: "The vital force is not enclosed in man, but radiates round him like a luminous sphere, and it may be made to act at a distance. In these semi-natural rays the imagination of man may produce healthy or morbid effects. It may poison the essence of life and cause diseases, or it may purify it after it has been made impure, and restore the health."[39]

The most common concept of the aura that we have today comes from the work of Dr. Walter J. Kilner (1847-1920) who published the results of his experiments into the nature of the aura in a book titled *The Human Atmosphere* (1911). By placing a dye made from coal tar between two sheets of glass, Kilner believed that he was able to make the aura visible. He would look through the dye screen in strong daylight, then immediately turn his gaze upon the naked body of a subject, who stood before a dark background in a dimly lit room.

KILNER'S THREE AURAS

Using this method, Kilner distinguished three auric layers. The first, called by Kilner the etheric double, was colorless and projected from the surface of the skin no more than from one quarter to one half inch. The second layer, called the inner aura, extended out from the body three inches. The third layer, called the outer aura, extended about twelve inches away from the skin.

Kilner discovered that the aura could be influenced by an electromagnetic field, chemical vapors and hypnosis of the subject. Sickness and a loss of the mental faculties reduced its strength. Mental illness altered its appearance. An effort of will on the part of the subject was able to change the color of the aura and project it farther away from the surface of the body. As death approached, it shrank closer to the skin. No aura was visible around a corpse.

THEOSOPHY'S FIVE AURAS

This model of the aura as three nesting shells of energy is complex enough for most of us, but the Theosophists were not content with it. They divided the aura into five fields that are not separate, but interpenetrate each other. A good scryer, they affirmed, is able to distinguish between these mingled energy fields. The five kinds of aura described by Theosophy are:

The Health Aura
This is almost colorless, but can be distinguished by the fine, straight lines of force that radiate outward

from the surface of the body like long, transparent hairs or filaments.

The Vital Aura

This circulates within the astral body and can be controlled to some extent by an act of will. It is a delicate rose color near the skin but changes to a pale blue farther out from the body.

The Karmic Aura

This is the aura of the animal or physical soul, the occult mirror upon which every sensation and desire is reflected. Changes in emotion are immediately expressed in the colors of this aura, which shift through the spectrum to mirror the feelings. It is this aura that is commonly observed by psychics.

The Character Aura

This aura is said to contain a complete record of the personality throughout the life of the individual.

The Spiritual Aura

This aura is seldom seen, but in those with a strong and refined spiritual nature it can outshine the other four auras and exhibit a brilliant radiance. It corresponds to the glory of saints.

Appearance of the Aura

The usual description of the aura is that of an oval or egg that surrounds the entire human body from head to foot, and can extend outward from the skin to a distance of several feet. Sometimes the aura is described as a sphere about six feet in diameter. Occasionally it is said to resemble a second skin that lies around the body like a cloak of colored light. If we are to believe the complex Theosophical model, we might explain this diversity of opinion by speculating that at times one form of the aura is seen, at other times a different form, leading to conflicting descriptions.

THE AURA IS NOT AN ENERGY FIELD

There is no scientific evidence for the existence of the aura as an energy field that can be measured and recorded by machines. Energy fields have been measured around the human body, but these do not correspond with descriptions of the aura. The aura is a sensory metaphor presented to the awareness of the scryer by the agents of his or her deep mind to express in perceivable terms information about the subject that has been acquired by extrasensory means.

PSYCHOLOGY OF THE AURA

You look at another person with the desire to know more about that individual. Your unconscious mind, perhaps aided by the spirits who dwell there, acquires the information you seek in ways that transcend your senses, or uses aspects of your senses of which you are not consciously aware. In order to make this raw data available to your conscious mind, your unconscious translates it into moving colors around the body of the person.

When I say that your unconscious may be using aspects of your physical senses that are below the level of your awareness to acquire this data, I mean that some of the information you perceive as the aura may come from such things as facial expressions, intonations of voice, body language, small gestures, body odors, and details of clothing that you do not consciously realize that you have perceived. What percentage of the aura derives from sensory data below the level of your conscious awareness, and what percentage comes from extrasensory data acquired directly by your deep mind, I do not pretend to know, but I believe that auras are based on a combination of the two sources.

INTERPRETING COLORS IN THE AURA

The meanings of the aura colors are the same that were given for the colors of the thought-forms that arise within the magic mirror. C. W. Leadbeater writes: "the meaning to be attached to them [the colors] is just the same in the thought-form as in the body out of which it is evolved."[40]

Briefly, it may be stated that a rosy aura indicates feelings of friendship and genuine affection, bright red indicates anger and the threat of violence, dark red expresses sensuality, orange is an indication of pride and ambition, bright yellow of intellectual activity, brown of avarice, dark green expresses jealousy and deceit, light green expresses sympathy, greenish yellow criticism, blue different degrees of devotion, and violet spirituality and psychic ability. Consult the more detailed list of colors provided in Chapter Fifteen on the magic mirror.

TEST YOUR AURA SCRYING ABILITY

Not everyone can see the aura. Merely because you can scry in the crystal and the black mirror, or have success using the pendulum and Ouija board, does not necessarily mean that you will be able to see the color envelope that surrounds all living things. For example, my brother sees auras quite clearly, but I can see them only with difficulty and under certain conditions. I find it easiest to see the aura in still air at twilight. Even then, I do not see colors, but only a shimmering field of energy that is similar to the waves of heat the rise from the hood of a car on a hot summer day.

You may wish to test your ability to perceive the aura. The easiest way to do this is to go into a room where the light is very dim. You should be able to make out the shape of the furniture, but should not be able to see bright colors. Wait at least ten minutes in the semi-darkness. The air will take on a slightly granular appearance. This indicates that your night vision has been activated by the low light level.

Hold up your hand about two feet away from your face and look closely at the tips of your fingers. Do not look at the fingers themselves, but at the air just beyond the ends of your nails. After a while you should see streams of what appear to be extremely fine particles, like microscopic black dust, flowing out from your fingertips. It makes the air at the ends of your fingers shimmer and dance. This is an aspect of your own aura.

BARON VON REICHENBACH

This aura was observed by Baron von Reichenbach in 1840, who also noticed that some individuals could see luminous emanations from magnets and rock crystals under conditions of darkness. He recorded the observation of reddish yellow flame from the south pole of magnets and bluish green flame from the north pole. His findings were published in 1848 in a work translated into English two years later under the title *Researches on Magnetism, Electricity, Heat, Light, Crystallisation and Chemical Attraction in their Relations to the Vital Force.*

Reichenbach called this magnetic emanation od, or odyllic, force. In addition to observing it flow from the human body, magnets and crystals, he asserted that it was also present in the rays of the Sun and the Moon, a possible explanation why the Moon strengthens the scrying ability and the Sun weakens it. Presumably the odyllic forces in the Sun and Moon are of opposite polarities, and it is the lunar polarity that acts as the medium for the transfer of extrasensory information.

FRIEDRICH ANTON MESMER

I can find no significant difference between the odyllic force of Reichenbach and the animal magnetism of Friedrich Anton Mesmer (1733-1815). Mesmer also believed this occult energy to be present in the rays of the planets and the bodies of human beings. He linked it to magnetism, and observed that it could be manipulated and controlled by magnets, the human voice, and the human will.

Mesmer enjoyed remarkable success in healing hysteria, depression, and other mental ills, probably because his methods relied on hypnotically induced suggestion coupled with a strong expectation of a cure in the minds of his patients. The same might be said of the healing miracles of Jesus, Simon Magus, or any other charismatic healer. Mesmer was able to activate the powers of the unconscious minds of his patients, enabling them in many cases to heal themselves.

The error of Mesmer and Reichenbach lay in maintaining that this nerve-energy was physical. When their experiments were subjected to scientific testing, no evidence for a physical force could be detected, and both men were discredited publicly. Their error was understandable. The aura does appear to be a physical light to those with the ability to see it. There was no reason for these psychics to doubt the evidence of their own senses. If they could see it with their eyes, they naturally assumed it must exist.

They did not realize that the aura was a sensory metaphor generated by the deep mind for the purpose of communicating with the conscious awareness. This was well before the revelations of Sigmund Freud and Carl Jung concerning the complexities of the mind. There was no way for Mesmer or Reichenbach to suspect the layers of complexity that lie hidden beneath everyday human awareness, or that intelligences dwelling within these depths could manipulate the physical senses.

THOUGHT-FORM EMANATIONS FROM THE AURA

In addition to the colors of the aura, you should look for shapes emitted from the aura under conditions of intense emotion. Annie Besant and C. W. Leadbeater mention the case of a drunken man in London's East End who struck his wife. A Theosophist observed that the instant before he hit the woman, a jagged bolt of red light flashed out of a dark cloud from his aura.[41]

A central sphere of gold radiating rose-colored

wings emitted from the aura of one person toward another indicates an attitude of protectiveness and benediction. Numerous straight rays emitted from a rose aura in all directions show the conscious projection of universal love. Many curving hooks that extend out in one direction and bend back to re-enter the aura show a grasping or possessive affection.

A blue cloud over the head indicates general religious feeling. When flecked with gray or brown, it shows that this devotional emotion is mingled with fear or selfishness. Strongly directed prayer exhibits itself as a bright blue cone with its point upward. A vague yellow cloud shows intellectual pleasure, but an undulation or corkscrew of yellow light projected from the aura indicates a questing desire to learn the answer to some puzzle. Curving hooks of orange indicate ambition for power. When these hooks turn a dull brownish or greyish orange and extend in all directions, selfish ambition of a general kind is revealed.

Explosive anger is indicated by a star burst of red and yellow rays. Jealous suspicion takes the form of a brownish green serpent that seems to be questing out with its head raised on its curved neck. When this suspicion turns to angry certainty, the serpent is transformed into a brownish green cloud rent by red rays of fury. A general emotion of sympathy is expressed by a pale green cloud.

Fear is shown by gray fragments of the aura that are thrown off like a spray of pebbles. Selfish greed expresses itself through a projection from the aura of a cluster of barbed hooks that are muddy-green in color. The strong desire for alcohol takes a similar shape, but is a dirty and mottled red. The lowest type

of perverse sexual desire also shows itself as projecting tendrils with barbed hooks on their ends, but of a
darker red.

AURA READING A SUBJECTIVE ART

Only your own experience will show whether these
Theosophical thought-forms projected from the aura
are valid. You may discover that human emotions
take different shapes in your visual perception. If you
are fortunate enough to see auras, you will learn to
interpret the various colors and projections over time
through trial and error. Often the meaning of a particular color or shape will be confirmed shortly after
by the behavior of the person who projects it. If you
attentively watch how individuals behave and compare their behavior with the manifestations of their
auras, you will soon arrive at a true understanding of
these manifestations.

CHAPTER 20

Psychometry

SCRYING OBJECTS BY TOUCH

Psychometry (Greek: "soul measuring") is the faculty of sensory automatism that allows a scryer to read the history and events surrounding an object by touch. Usually small personal objects are used, such as a watch, a ring, a key, a lock of hair, a letter, and so on. The scryer, called a psychometrist, either holds the object in the hands or presses it against the forehead. This is the origin of the cliché of the stage magician who pretends to "read" objects by pressing them to his brow.

THE FATHER OF PSYCHOMETRY

The term psychometry was invented in 1842 by J. Rhodes Buchanan (1814-1899). Buchanan was fascinated by the assertions of the Civil War general Bishop Polk that he was unusually sensitive to atmospheric and physical surroundings. Polk told Buchanan that if he touched a door handle in the dark, he immediately knew that it was brass by the unpleasant taste that came into his mouth.

Buchanan began to experiment with the help of students at a Cincinnati medical school, and discovered that some of them reacted in the same way when different medicines were handed to them as they would have responded had they taken the medicines internally. For example, when an emetic was handed to one student, he felt the overpowering urge to vomit, even though he had no knowledge of what the vessel contained.

BUCHANAN'S THEORY OF PSYCHOMETRY

Buchanan developed the theory that all things, including the human body, give off some form of emanation that certain sensitive persons are able to perceive and interpret in their normal conscious state. He called the emanation of the human body the nerve aura. These emanations contain a record of the history and surroundings of the object. Just as a photographic negative receives and retains an impression of an image that is shone upon it, which later may be transferred to a light sensitive paper to make a positive print, so Buchanan believed that physical objects recorded scenes and emotions, and that these could later be played back in the minds of psychometric scryers:

> The past is entombed in the present, the world is its own enduring monument; and that which is true of its physical is likewise true of its mental career. The discoveries of Psychometry will enable us to explore the history of man, as those of geology enable us to explore

the history of the earth. There are mental fossils for psychologists as well as mineral fossils for the geologists; and I believe that hereafter the psychologist and the geologist will go hand in hand, the one portraying the earth, its animals and its vegetation, while the other portrays the human beings who have roamed over its surface in the shadows, and the darkness of primeval barbarism.[42]

THE AKASHIC RECORDS

Theosophists attempted to explain psychometry in terms of the Akashic records, a nonphysical and imperishable medium upon which all mental and physical actions are recorded. This record is in theory available to all consciousness that has achieved a high enough level of perfection, but is only briefly and occasionally glimpsed by flawed human consciousness. This is a seductive theory, but it does not explain how some psychometric impressions have been received from the future.

One such psychometric premonition is recorded in the *Proceedings of the Society for Psychical Research*. A contributor writes of having seen in a vision a man drown himself while walking along the shore of a lake. A week later a man did commit suicide in the same place by jumping into the lake.[43]

If we are going to use the Akashic record explanation for psychometry, we must assume that the Akashic records exist outside of normal time and space, and give access to the future as well as the past. This is not such a strange speculation in these days when serious physicists and mathematicians write papers on space warps, subatomic time travel, ten-dimensional space, and alternate universes. However, it must have seemed a daring leap of reasoning in the age of Queen Victoria.

CONDITIONS HELPFUL TO PSYCHOMETRY

Most psychometrists scry in a normal state of consciousness. G. R. S. Mead writes: "It would be as well to have it understood that the method of investigation to which I am referring does not bring into consideration any question of trance, either self-induced, or mesmerically or hypnotically effected. As far as I can judge, my colleagues are to all outward seeming in quite their normal state. They go through no outward ceremonies, or internal ones for that matter, nor even any outward preparation but that of assuming a comfortable position."[44]

Hypnosis seems in some cases to heighten the force of the impressions received. It may aid in producing the necessary receptive state of mind for automatism. Scryers either naturally or hypnotically sensitive to psychometric impressions are sometimes unable to hold certain objects because of their repugnant or violent associations. They experience terror or even become physically sick. When handed an object that belonged to a person who has recently died, some scryers unconsciously take on the personal appearance and behavior of the departed, and even suffer from symptoms of the fatal disease.

NATURE OF PSYCHOMETRIC PERCEPTIONS

Psychometric impressions come in the form of physical sensations and spontaneous emotions, sounds, scents, tastes, and images. Often a very fleeting contact is enough to trigger them. The visions are rapid flashes that occur too swiftly in succession to write down as they happen. It is necessary to go over them later in the mind and sort them out to record their contents. The medium D'Aute-Hooper reported upon scrying a stone: "I seem to be the piece of stone, without thinking power but seeing things and happenings around me."[45]

Sometimes the images are tiny; at other times they appear to surround the scryer or fill the scrying chamber. The visual flashes occur with no logical sequence, like the chaotic images of a kaleidoscope, but the most significant images seem to endure longer and come more often.

METHOD OF STEPHAN OSSOWIECKI

The Polish psychometrist Stephan Ossowiecki reported concerning his own method:

> I begin by stopping all reasoning, and I throw all my inner power into perception of spiritual sensation.... I then find myself in a new and special state in which I see and hear outside time and space.... I seem to lose some energy; my temperature becomes febrile, and the heartbeats unequal. I am confirmed in this supposition because, as soon as I cease from reasoning, something like electricity flows through my extremities for a few seconds. This lasts a moment only, and then lucidity takes possession of me, pictures arise, usually of the past.... The vision is misty and needs great tension. Considerable effort is required to perceive some details and conditions of the scenes presented. The lucid state

sometimes arises in a few minutes, and sometimes it takes hours of waiting. This largely depends on the surroundings; skepticism, incredulity, or even attention too much concentrated on my person, paralyses quick success in reading or sensation.[46]

Ossowiecki's account of the psychometric experience is revealing. Notice that he stresses the suspension of his analytical reasoning and the entry into what he calls a "lucid state." Elsewhere Fodor writes concerning this condition: "The percipient is passive. The exercise of the faculty requires a lax, receptive mind." This is the receptive state of consciousness I have mentioned in connection with other forms of scrying. It is absolutely essential for any form of automatism, although it often becomes so automatic that scryers are not aware of any change in their consciousness.

It is also significant that Ossowiecki links this receptive state of mind with the transcendence of normal time and space. He says that in this state "pictures arise, usually of the past," implying that sometimes they are images of the present, or even the future. If the receptive mental state really is beyond time, encompassing all eternity in some durationless now, then the future should be just as easy to scry as the past. It is the expectation of the scryer that determines from which direction in time the sense impressions arise.

PHYSICAL EFFECTS OF PSYCHOMETRY

There are two physiological factors mentioned by Ossowiecki, both vitally important in understanding the psychometric process. The first is a loss of energy and an increase in body temperature, along with an irregularity of the heartbeat. The second is an electric energy that flows through the limbs for several seconds.

I can comment on these phenomena because I have often experienced them. When scrying, I frequently feel changes in body temperature. For me there is usually a subjective drop in temperature, not a rise, but less often I feel warmth and a sensation that is similar to prickly heat upon the surface of my skin. My heartbeat sometimes increases or becomes irregular, from time to time skipping a beat. There is often a strong sensation of lethargy, which is actually quite pleasant. It can be likened to an injection of some narcotic drug that suddenly flushes throughout the arteries and muscles of the body with a delightful relaxing and pleasurable feeling that brings on the desire to sleep. This may be what Ossowiecki means by a "loss of energy."

THE PSYCHIC DYNAMO

The electrical sensation is, unfortunately, indescribable. Nonetheless, I will do my best to convey it to you. It is preceded by an inner sense of gathering power, as though a vast dynamo were winding up to its peak rate of revolution and preparing to discharge all its energy in a single burst. To some extent, this release of energy into the body is under the control of the will. If I attempt to stop it, I can turn at least a portion of it aside and reduce its force. I usually have a few seconds premonition that it is coming before it hits me physically.

The first few times I received this energy burst I did attempt to divert it away from my body, because it is a frightening experience. I had no idea what this power was or where it came from. I felt as though my body were in danger of being overloaded by its potential, the way a wire will melt when too many amperes are forced through it. However, after I had experienced it several times without suffering any injury, I learned to open myself to receive it.

This energy flow is accompanied by a spinning, rushing sensation deep inside my center of being—the power vortex or dynamo that is the source of the electric discharge. Ossowiecki is correct in calling the sensation one of "electricity," although I would qualify his description by saying that it is a rapid, powerful vibration or oscillating pulse through the body of the type that is felt during an electric shock from alternating current. There is no pain involved.

The vibration is also similar to the return of sensation in an arm or leg that has "fallen asleep" and has begun to regain its feeling. It is akin to the sensation first experienced when the blood begins to flow, but before the onset of the pins and needles that are so unpleasant. There is nothing painful or unpleasant about this electric surge. It is frightening only because it is so incredibly powerful.

The electricity flows along the nerve paths from the center of the torso out through the limbs, gathering force as it does so until it reaches the fingers and toes, which seem to tingle very strongly. The last time I felt this flow, I was lying in bed. The gathering momentum of the central dynamo (as I think of it) alerted me to what was about to occur. I was able to observe quite clearly the route taken by the energy, which arose from somewhere in the center of my chest and branched into each of my arms to rush rapidly out to my fingers.

This particular burst of energy was confined to my upper body. It tingled along my arms and focused itself in my fingers, and I had the clear impression that streams of energy were flowing like great fountains of invisible fire from my fingertips. I allowed this to occur without attempting to suppress it. The energy flow was exactly equal from both hands. After about ten seconds it gradually dropped in intensity and ceased.

KUNDALINI FIRE

I have speculated in my own mind that the physical source of this energy is the spinal column, probably in the region of the heart center (although sometimes it seems to originate deep in the unconscious), and that it takes a path along the nerves to the extremities. Very likely this energy is similar, if not identical, to the fire of Kundalini that is awakened by the practice of Tantric yoga. It began to arise within me spontaneously after I had been practicing scrying and other forms of ritual magic on a daily basis for several months. It seems to be connected in some way with automatism, but I do not pretend to understand exactly what that connection accomplishes.

PSYCHOMETRY AND SPIRITS

Buchanan regarded psychometry as a natural power of the human mind and tended to dismiss the theory that it was controlled by spiritual beings. However, many psychics who use psychometry believe that they merely act as passive instruments, and that spirits do the actual scrying of the objects they hold or touch.

Seeing ghosts is an example of psychometry. Ghosts are usually confined to a specific place and often to a specific time of appearance as well. Instead of scrying an object, the person who sees or feels or hears a ghost scries the surrounding atmosphere of a place. According to one theory of spiritualism, ghosts are not the earthbound souls of the dead, but merely images recorded upon physical localities, such as the rooms of certain houses, by an unusually powerful emotional event such as a suicide or murder. If this is true, someone who sees a ghost is unconsciously reading the local surroundings upon which this emotional image has been imprinted.

The Scrying of History

One fascinating use of psychometry is the reading of the Akashic records to learn unknown events in history or recover lost works of literature. The first book based entirely on consciously scried information is W. Scott-Elliott's *The Story of Atlantis*. Another is G. R. S. Mead's *Did Jesus Live 100 B.C.?*, which contains passages from lost Greek manuscripts scried through psychometry.

Attempts have been made, some apparently successful, to reconstruct details in the lives of great historical figures such as Alexander the Great and Julius Caesar through physical contact with some object believed to have once been in their possession, or through a relic from their corpse. Similar efforts have gone into reconstructing the archaeological details of ancient sites such as Stonehenge and Glastonbury Tor. Needless to say, science wants nothing to do with such unorthodox methods, and historical and archaeological scryers are forced to pretend that their findings are the result of more conventional methods of research.

AWAKENING YOUR PSYCHOMETRIC TALENT

If you possess a talent for psychometry, you probably already know it. Those who receive visual and other sensory impressions from physical objects and places usually do so at an early age. However, conscious and deliberate practice can strengthen an existing talent that has remained dormant for years, or been suppressed out of fear.

One way to practice this talent is to find objects with a known history that is unknown to you. If possible, take them into your scrying chamber and handle them upon your scrying table within the sphere of light after your third eye has been activated. Close your eyes. Press the object gently against your forehead over your third eye and hold it there for a dozen seconds or so with both hands. Allow your mind to enter a receptive state. Do not attempt to force impressions—allow them to arise naturally without criticizing them with your rational mind.

Whatever impressions you receive from the object, record them in detail in your scrying journal. Then, after you have scried the object, do whatever research you can into its history. The best objects to work with are family heirlooms that have been passed down through the generations. These will have strong associations, and with luck someone in your family will know something about them that you can compare with your own scried visions. The second best objects for practice in psychometry are museum artifacts. These you must scry in situ before you attempt to learn their history. Afterwards, you can research the objects in the museum records.

William Denton, a professor of geology who did independent research into the findings of J. R. Buchanan, asserted that one man in ten and four women in ten possess some degree of psychometric ability. These percentages are no more than an estimate and should not be taken too seriously. All of those who have shown mediumistic skill in other areas are said to have this talent to a greater or lesser extent. The regular practice of other forms of scrying, such as the use of the crystal and the black mirror, coupled with the visualization exercises given earlier, should help to awaken this talent for object reading if it is latent in your nature.

CHAPTER 21

Dowsing

THE WORKHORSE OF SCRYING

Of all the forms of automatism, the most widely accepted and used for practical day-to-day purposes is dowsing. This folk method for finding things lost or hidden under the surface of the earth has been passed down within families and communities from generation to generation for many centuries. In spite of the unceasing ridicule heaped upon it by scientists and skeptics, it has continued to survive, and even to flourish, because it is perceived to give useful results.

At one time there was no other way to determine the best location to dig a well than the dowsing rod. Even with modern technology, locating a well can be a hit or miss affair. A few feet left or right can make the difference between a constant, high-volume flow and a trickle. Modern well drillers often employ dowsers (also called water-witches) not just for water wells but when sinking oil and natural gas wells.

Dowsing is routinely employed to locate buried pipes and electrical cables whose exact position has been forgotten. Dinosaur hunters have relied on it to discover fossilized bones. Archaeologists have followed the dowsing rod to track the position of buried foundations. Mining engineers dowse mineral deposits both out in the field and upon the surface of geological survey maps. Treasure hunters dowse the sites of sunken wrecks.

THE VIRGULA FURCATA

Although mention is made in the writings of classical Rome to a *virgula divina* (divining rod), this instrument had no connection with the dowsing rod. Roman divining rods were single lengths of wood cast during divination and interpreted according to how they fell. The dowsing rod is the *virgula furcata* (forked rod), which received this name due to its customarily forked shape.

Descriptions of the rod vary. Most commonly it is made from a branch of hazel that forks equally to form a shape similar to the capital letter Y. Its overall length may vary from six to thirty inches, but it is always cut from a living tree and thin enough to be springy and flexible in the hands. An older source in my library (1751) specifies that the rod should be cut during the winter months, but another source (1819) states just the opposite, saying: "They are not so fit for the use of the diviner in winter, or when dry, being less flexible."[47]

DOWSING FOR MINERALS

The virgula furcata appears to have been first used by German miners to discover new lodes of ore in the sixteenth century. It is described by Georg Agricola

(1490–1555) in his famous textbook on mining techniques, *De re Metallica* (1556). From Germany it was carried to England when Cornish mine owners imported expert German miners from the Harz Mountains during the reign of Queen Elizabeth I to take advantage of their advanced techniques. The Germans called the dowsing rod a *schlagruthe* ("striking-rod") because of the way it suddenly twisted downward when carried over a deposit of ore.

The divining rod is first mentioned explicitly in England in 1663 in an essay by the father of chemistry, Robert Boyle, who wrote: "A forked hazel twig is held by its horns, one in each hand, the holder walking with it over places where mineral lodes may be suspected, and it is said that the fork by dipping down will discover the place where the ore is to be found.... When visiting the lead-mines of Somersetshire I saw its use, and one gentleman who employed it declared that it moved without his will, and I saw it bend so strongly as to break in his hand. It will only succeed in some men's hands, and those who have seen it may much more readily believe than those who have not."[48]

DOWSING FOR WATER IN FRANCE

The earliest recorded use of the dowsing rod to discover water occurred around 1630 in France. It was not employed for this purpose in England until a century later, when the mines in Cornwall began to play out and dowsers had to discover some other employment for their talent. The Abbot Deramel is said to have discovered 10,275 underground water sources with the wand. In 1853 the French Academy of Sciences delegated a commission to investigate the dowsing rod, and concluded that it moved by involuntary and unconscious muscular action on the part of the dowser.

TRADITIONAL FORMS OF THE DOWSING ROD

In addition to the forked hazel wand, two straight hazel wands may be bound together with thread several inches down their lengths and spread apart into the shape of an irregular X. When the longer legs are grasped in the hands and flexed, the action is similar to that of a forked wand.

The other traditional form of the dowsing rod is a single hazel wand that is bent between the hands into the form of a taunt bow. This not only bends downward, but actually revolves between the hands when held over a water source. The bowed rod of a French dowser named Bleyton spun at a rate of eighty revolutions per minute. In 1876 an English landowner employed a young boy to dowse for water on his property using this bowed kind of wand. He watched the boy and later described what took place:

He immediately repaired to a neighbouring hedge, and returned with a rod of blackthorn or hazel—I think the former—about 2 ft. 3 in. in length, and of the thickness of telegraph wire. Then, placing the ends of the rod between the thumb and forefinger of each hand, bending it slightly, and holding it before him at a short distance from the ground, he started on his expedition; I and others following him, and watching every movement closely. After going up and down, crossing and recrossing the ground several times, but never on the same lines, the lad stopped, and to our great surprise we saw the rod exhibit signs of motion, the fingers and thumbs being perfectly motionless. The motion or trembling of the rod increasing, it slowly began to revolve, then at an accelerated pace, fairly twisting itself to such an extent that the lad, although he tried his best to retain it, was obliged to let it go, and it fled to some distance.[49]

The motions of the divining rod—its sudden breaking in the hands, its rapid revolution, and its flying completely out of the hands some distance through the air—occur quite often in historical descriptions of the practice. It is often stated that the rod moved so violently that it could not be held.

How the Rod Moves

There can be little question that the motion of the rod comes from the hands of the person using it. A freshly cut wand of hazel has no power to independently spin around or fly through the air. It is equally certain that the dowser is completely unconscious of moving the rod, just as those who use the Ouija board do not realize that they are moving the planchette. The movement of the dowsing rod is the most common, and probably the easiest to achieve, of all types of automatism.

A dowser has a specific purpose in mind. It may be the discovery of an underground spring, or a lost object, or a buried cable. This conscious willed intention communicates itself to the deep mind, which extends itself through its agents to acquire the desired information. The deep mind communicates the information to the dowser by causing the arms and hands of the dowser to move slightly in a way that brings about the desired response in the wand. For the best results, the wand must be held under tension so that a very small relaxation of the hands produces a large movement in the end of the wand.

The best material for the wand, forked or straight, is hazel or blackthorn. Other woods used are white-thorn, holly, beech, apple, and especially for water-finding, the willow, which is the most water-loving of all trees. It is important that the bark have some roughness so that it can be held under tension in the hands without twisting prematurely, and that the wand be flexible enough not to break when bent and springy enough to seek to return to its original shape.

UNCONVENTIONAL TYPES OF ROD

Other traditional materials used include copper wire, steel wire, and straightened watch spring. One English dowser working in 1812 told his patron that "a steel rod was as good or better than the hazel rod."[50] Modern dowsers often use two lengths of steel wire bent into an L shape and held loosely in the fists with the thumbs uppermost so that the horizontal leg of the wires extends forward over the index finger. When a water source or other dowsed object is encountered, these wires turn simultaneously outward or inward in the hands. Sometimes these wires are supported in short lengths of tubing held in the fists to allow them to turn more easily.

A few dowsers who are unusually sensitive do not use any wand at all. They rely on sensations in their hands and arms to alert them when they are standing over whatever it is they seek. Describing the method of one such dowser, a Miss Goodrich Freer wrote: "His hands, hung down, extended a little outwards, and on observing closely, we could see, from time to time a vibration in the middle fingers which appeared to be drawn downwards, just as in the case of the apex of the twig."[51] The Abbe Bouly stated during a lecture in 1928: "I no longer require a rod, I can see the stream with my eyes; I attune my mind; I am looking for lead, I fix my eyes; I feel a wavy sensation like hot air over a radiator; I see it."[52]

SENSATIONS EXPERIENCED WHEN DOWSING

The sensations experienced during dowsing are subtle and easily missed, but quite distinct. As the object dowsed is approached, the arms and legs tingle and sometimes tremble or twitch. Perspiration may break out, and the dowser may experience a slight dizziness. This comes to its peak when the dowser actually puts a foot upon the exact spot where the wand turns. If the dowser keeps walking past the spot, these symptoms disappear.

HOW TO HOLD THE ROD

There are three main ways to hold the wand. When using a forked wand, the two angled branches, or horns, are held in front of the body at waist level in the fists with the thumbs outward and the fingers uppermost, so that the ends of the horns project past the thumbs an inch or so. The ends of the horns are bent apart so that the ends point in opposite directions in a straight line that extends through both hands, and the point of the wand is inclined upward at an angle of about eighty degrees to the horizon.

When the dowser approaches the object of the search, the end of the wand lifts slightly as though pressing against some invisible barrier. But when the dowser actually steps on the spot itself, the end of the wand twists down sharply and points at the ground. Sometimes this motion is so forceful that the wand will snap. Some dowsers who use the virgula fircata say that the end of the wand twists up for water and down for ore, but this appears to be only a superstition.

The second method of holding the wand involves the use of a single, flexible hazel wand. This is pinched lightly at the ends between the thumbs and forefingers of both hands, and pressed between the hands using the balls of the thumbs against the ends until it bends strongly upward. When the object of the search is approached, the wand vibrates and revolves downward, sometimes spinning completely around between the hands, or even flying completely out of the grasp.

The third method of holding the wand involves the use of two separate rods or wires that are bent into an L-shape. As I described above, these are supported loosely in the extended fists with the knuckles of the thumbs on top, so that the horizontal legs of the wires hang outward over the longest joints of the index fingers. Short lengths of pipe or tubing held in the fists allow the wires, which are set into them, to rotate more freely. These wires act in unison just as though they were connected by some invisible link, and usually turn in opposite directions, either outward together or inward together.

WHAT CAN BE DOWSED

Apparently anything under the Sun can be dowsed. It is traditionally believed that metal is easier to locate than water. Some metals appear to draw the rod more strongly than others, although there is no firm consensus on this point. Generally it may be said that gold draws more strongly than silver, followed by tin, lead, and copper. Curiously enough, nickel exerts a powerful attraction that may be second only to gold, or even greater than gold.

Other strange things that have been dowsed successfully include graves, caves, buried treasure, ancient temples, lost rings, lost persons, the site of diseases inside the human body, shipwrecks, and the whereabouts of criminals. In 1692 a French diviner named Jacques Aymar used his divining rod like a psychic bloodhound to track the murderers of a Lyons wine seller and his wife. One of the murderers was traced by this method to a prison where he was serving time for another crime. He confessed to killing the wine merchant.[53]

The most curious aspect of dowsing is that it can be done successfully using only a map. This is conclusive proof that it is the unconscious mind that supplies the movement to the rod, not some occult attraction between the rod and the object dowsed. Map dowsing was being used as early as 1913, when Joseph Mathieu claimed this ability at the International Congress of Experimental Psychology at Paris. In modern times it is commonly employed to locate the sites of sunken treasure ships, to discover rich deposits of ore, coal, or oil, and to find individuals or planes lost in the wilderness.

DOWSING WITH THE PENDULUM

The pendulum is frequently employed in place of the more traditional dowsing wand of wood or metal. Natural rock crystals suspended on silver chains are popular. This is not so modern a practice as might be initially suspected. In 1930 the famous psychic investigator and ghost hunter Harry Price observed the pendulum method of the French dowser Abbe Gabriel Lambert, who employed a cone-shaped bobbin, painted with bright, striped colors, on the end of a piece of thread. This he held out in his right hand.

Lambert would walk forward swinging the bobbin from side to side. Price tested him by asking him to dowse for an underground stream in Hyde Park, London. When he came near his target, the bobbin, according to Price, "would make a spasmodic movement, change its course, and commence spinning furiously, describing a larger and larger circle the longer we stood over the source of activity. When we reached the bank of the subterranean river the bobbin would stop dead—just as if it had been hit by a stone."[54]

HOW TO BECOME A SKILLED "DEWSTER"

You do not need to work outside to learn to become a skilled dewster, as dowsers used to be called in England. Cut a forked wand of hazel, willow, or some other flexible wood with a rough bark and try different grips and pressures while approaching a basin of water or an object of silver or gold. It is important that you know in advance what substance your are dowsing. Those who dowse for oil or minerals often walk over underground springs without the slightest movement in the wand. Tell your unconscious what you are dowsing for, and it will activate the wand when you approach that substance.

If you do not have access to hazel wands, practice with bent pieces of wire held loosely in the hands. Sections of heavy coat-hanger wire work well. These should be bent at a right angle near the middle, and balanced in such a way that they rock freely across the longest joint of your index finger when you hold them loosely inside your fist.

You may want to experiment with sliding weights on the projecting ends of the angled wire to achieve this balance. You can accomplish this by wrapping a small piece of thinner copper wire around the projecting ends, and sliding this coil back and forth until you find the ideal balance point.

To make the swinging of the wire to the left and right easier, try cutting short lengths of thin copper pipe and holding these in your fists with the angled wires sitting inside the pipes. In order for this to work, the rim of the pipe must be completely smooth. If the end of the pipe is rough, the wire will not rotate properly. Personally, I prefer to cradle the wires in my bare hands. There is a greater sensitivity this way.

Hold whatever substance you intend to dowse against your third eye and concentrate on sensing its nature. Then set it down in some convenient place on the open floor and approach it slowly with the dowsing rod, or rods, in your hands. Take it slowly. You will have to experiment with different ways of holding the rod, but when success comes it will probably come quite strongly and leave little doubt in your mind. Many people who have been shown how to hold the rod by expert dowsers get results on their very first attempt.

Dowsing is probably the easiest form of scrying, or automatism, with the possible exception of the pendulum. Even persons with no other psychic ability often discover that they are excellent dowsers. This is a very useful talent that will bring you great pride in achievement if you learn the technique. Once learned, it is yours forever. As is true of all forms of scrying, the power of dowsing lies within your own mind, and is not dependent on any outside instrument.

CHAPTER 22

Automatic Writing

WHAT IS AUTOMATIC WRITING?

Automatic writing is one of the most useful scrying techniques, but also one of the rarest and most difficult. It falls into the category of motor automatism, where the deep mind delivers its information to the everyday awareness by taking control of the nerves and muscles of a part of the body below the level of consciousness—in this case, the nerves and muscles that control the arm and hand.

When using the Ouija board, movements of the hand upon the planchette point out words and sentences on a lettered board. In the case of automatic writing, the planchette is used upon a sheet of blank paper with a pencil inserted into its pointed end to write words directly upon the paper. More skilled automatic writers (called autonographists) hold the pencil directly in their hand while they write, eliminating the need for the planchette.

Never Let Your Right Hand Know What Your Left Is Doing

Many of the phenomena of automatic writing are similar to those already described for other forms of automatism. The autonographist must achieve an abstracted, receptive state of awareness. It is important not to focus the awareness on the hand holding the planchette or pencil, or to pay any conscious attention to what is being written. The moment consciousness is focused on the message, the writing will cease. Consciousness blocks the reception of data from the unconscious.

The medium Stainton Moses used to receive automatic writing with his left hand while at the same time writing his regular correspondence with his right hand. Many autonographists hold verbal conversations with others in the room while they write unconsciously. After a high level of skill has been achieved, it is possible to look at the hand producing the automatic script, and even to read some of what is being written, but if the scryer focuses too much attention on the content of the writing, it will become disconnected, with words left out, or incoherent, or altogether cease.

Method of Working

The easiest way to begin is with the writing planchette. This differs from the pointer used with the Ouija board in that it has two rear legs, but in place of the front leg a pencil is inserted through a hole in the end of the pointer. Set the planchette over a large sheet of blank paper. It is best to tape this sheet down to the table so that it will not move around. The motions of the planchette can at times become vigorous. You should experiment with placing the fingertips of both hands on the planchette, then either hand individually, to discover which works best.

If you do not own a writing planchette, you can try holding the pencil in your bare hand, just as you do when writing. Again, the paper should be taped down, or you should use a large artist's drawing pad. Some autonographists find it necessary to have someone else in the room to insert a new sheet of paper under the hand when the first becomes full. However, with practice you may find that you can allow enough attention to go to your writing hand to alert you when the first sheet is full so that you can change the sheets with your opposite hand.

PRELIMINARY MOVEMENTS ARE SOMETIMES VIOLENT

The sensations that come immediately prior to automatic writing may be so slight that they pass unnoticed. You may discover after sitting with the pencil in your hand for several minutes that you have written words without even being aware that the pencil had moved. On the other hand, the preliminary sensations and movements of the hand can be powerful and even violent. You should not allow this to frighten you.

The medium Stainton Moses describes his first experience with automatic writing:

> My right arm was seized about the middle of the forearm, and dashed violently up and down with a noise resembling that of a number of paviors at work. It was

the most tremendous exhibition of "unconscious muscular action" I ever saw. In vain I tried to stop it. I distinctly felt the grasps, soft and firm, round my arm, and though perfectly possessed of senses and volition, I was powerless to interfere, although my hand was disabled for some days by the bruising it then got. The object we soon found was to get up the force.[55]

The experience of Stainton Moses is more violent than most, but by no means uncommon. What he means by "get up the force" is to establish a channel of direct control between the agent or agents of the unconscious mind responsible for the writing and the muscles of the arm and hand that writes. Another medium, William Hewitt, experienced what he described as an "electric shock" run down through his arm to his hand after he had sat holding the pencil for several minutes. Then his arm began to make increasingly large and vigorous circles in the air for about ten minutes. At last the arm came to rest on the paper, and the pencil began to write.

YOGIC HOPPING

Those who study advanced techniques of yoga will be perfectly familiar with this type of automatic muscular action. One sign of success during intense meditation is automatic motions of the muscles of the body. Yogis sitting in the lotus position have often been known to involuntarily hop across the floor like frogs. More commonly, they experience strong movements in their arms and legs, or grimaces in the face. Sometimes they make involuntary noises in their throats.

Their gurus explain that this is caused by the

circulation of the energy of Kundalini through the esoteric nerve channels of the body. As the Kundalini force opens each new channel, it produces an involuntary movement in the associated muscles. It is perfectly natural and quite harmless. As meditation progresses, these movements vanish.

TOUCH OF SPIRITS VERY REAL

It is interesting that Stainton Moses mentions the sensation of hands grasping his arm. I have felt similar touches upon various parts of my body during ritual work, and can state emphatically to those who may be doubtful about the reality of such things that these pressures do indeed feel exactly like the touch of invisible hands. When you experience this curious sensation, there will remain no doubt in your mind concerning its nature. Feeling is believing.

Whether these sensations are caused by independent, conscious, discarnate beings or produced by the unconscious self of the scryer is a moot point. I can tell you that they feel like the touches of spirits. What these spirits are, and where they come from, is a more difficult question to answer.

THE NATURE OF SPIRITS

In my opinion, spirits are autonomous or semi-autonomous conscious beings who dwell in the depths of the unconscious mind. Their environment is the same one that we experience during our dreams. When we wake up, we exit this dream world, but the world continues to exist in our deep minds, and these spirits continue to inhabit it.

Occasionally, spirits notice the existence of our conscious selves, in the same way the wild animals of the forest will notice a person who comes to the same place each day with food for them. They begin to anticipate the rituals we practice to achieve a communication with them, and after a time will come more readily when these rituals are initiated. The attraction for them is our conscious attention and feelings of affection and love.

It may be that these spirits are themselves sensory metaphors created by our deep minds for the purpose of conveying information gathered by extrasensory means to our conscious awareness. By this I mean that just as the deep mind can cast its data into the form of sounds or images and send them to our awareness when we open it with a receptive mental state, so perhaps can the deep mind create independent, intelligent beings to act as its messengers. These spirit messengers (another word for them is "angels") are able to communicate the data of the deep mind to us in the form of direct conversation. This allows the deep mind to respond to our questions and desire for additional clarifications.

DIFFICULTY OF AUTOMATIC WRITING

The spirit calling itself F. W. H. Myers, who communicated several published books through the medium Geraldine Cummins by automatic writing, gives the following reasons that this talent is comparatively rare, even among those who have demonstrated advanced psychic abilities in other areas:

The inner mind is very difficult to deal with from this side. We impress it with our message. We never impress the brain of the medium directly. That is out of the question. But the inner mind receives our message and sends it on to the brain. The brain is a mere mechanism. The inner mind is like soft wax, it receives our thoughts, their whole content, but it must produce the words that clothe it. That is what makes cross-correspondence so very difficult. We may succeed in sending the thought through, but the actual words depend largely on the inner mind's content, on what words will frame the thought.[56]

The "inner mind" referred to by the spirit Myers would seem to be what I have called here the deep mind or unconscious. The "brain" of Myers appears to be the same as the faculty of rational consciousness. Myers states that the unconscious must "produce the words that clothe" the thought messages of spirits. This refers to the production within the unconscious of what I have called sensory metaphors to express the data acquired by extrasensory means in terms the rational consciousness can understand. In the case of automatic writing, these sensory metaphors take the form of written words.

SPIRITS CAN READ THOUGHTS IN THE UNCONSCIOUS

It is interesting that Myers says that the messages of spirits impressed upon the wax of the inner, or deep, mind are transmitted to the deep mind all at once on a level below that of articulated words. This observation rings true in my own experience. As I have already mentioned, when I communicate with spirits, I have observed that they receive my thoughts before I actually am able to express them in the form of mental words. They seem able to snatch the proto-thought directly out of my deep mind, where it initially forms, before I have the chance to articulate it in words even to my own rational consciousness.

Whatever spirits are, they behave as independent, intelligent beings with their own likes and dislikes, their own purposes, their own thoughts and feelings. For the best results when dealing with them, this is the way spirits should be treated. If it walks like a duck and quacks like a duck, treat it as a duck, at least until you know with greater certainty that it is something else.

The Quality of Automatic Writing

At first, the movements of the pencil will be small circles or short, vertical lines. You must allow your hand to perform the automatic writing by itself. There is no use attempting to help it by forcing it into motion. This will only block the directing control of the agents of your unconscious mind. Strong, random movements of the hand are a very good sign. They indicate that your deep mind is taking control and opening the nerve pathways it needs to produce writing. A tingling in your arm and hand is also a good sign.

Automatic writing is seldom clear and elegant. The words may run together without breaks between them. Sometimes they slant right off the edge of the paper. Sometimes they are so small they must be read with the aid of a magnifying glass. On rarer occasions, the words may be written in mirror inversion (called strephographia), or in the reverse order of the letters ("cat" would be written "tac"), or even upside down. Do not assume that you have received nothing if the marks on the paper at first glance appear to make no sense. Analyze them, and put them away in a safe place for future reference.

Two Kinds of Automatic Writing

There are two forms of automatic writing. These are always treated together, but are quite different from each other in the psychological mechanisms that are involved. The first is the form we have been examining—a direct motor control of the writing instrument by the agents of the unconscious mind. The second form of automatic writing arrives as mental dictation. The autonographist hears these words as though they were spoken, or receives them strongly in the conscious mind, and copies them down just as a stenographer would record a letter dictated by her employer.

This is the way the infamous magician Aleister Crowley received his greatest work, *The Book of the Law,* which was dictated to him psychically in Cairo, Egypt, in 1904. On a personal note, it is also the method that I used to receive a set of twenty-four poems concerning the runes of the German rune alphabet. These poems were delivered to me individually on consecutive nights at the same hour each night. I recorded them exactly as they appeared in my mind. You will find them at the back of my book *Rune Magic.*

Some autonographists have carried their ability to a very high level. T. P. James, an American mechanic of limited education, completed the novel *The Mystery of Edwin Drood,* which its author, Charles

Dickens, had left unfinished at his death. A fourteen-year-old French girl named Hermance Dufeaux wrote two complete books, *Life of Jeanne d'Arc* and *Confessions of Louis XI*, both said to be of considerable merit. In our own time the books of Jane Roberts, which are dictated by a spirit who calls itself Seth, form a conspicuous body of this class of literature.

AUTOMATIC DRAWING

Very closely related to automatic writing is automatic drawing and painting. The method of working is very similar, as are the phenomena experienced at the beginning of a drawing. After trying for weeks to produce an automatic drawing without result, William Wilkinson writes of his sudden success:

> After waiting less than five minutes it began to move, at first slowly, but presently with increased speed, till in less than a quarter-of-an-hour it moved with such velocity as I had never seen in a hand and arm before, or since. It literally ran away in spiral forms; and I can compare it to nothing else than the fly-wheel of an engine when it was "run away." This lasted until a gentleman present touched my arm, when suddenly it fell like an infant's as it goes to sleep, and the pencil dropped out of my hand. I had, however, acquired the power. The consequences of the violent motion of the muscles of the arm were so apparent that I could not for several days lift it without pain.[57]

The products of automatic writing and drawing share several features in common. They are usually characterized by a fineness of detail and a polished style. The sentences of the writing are intricate and use elaborate grammatical constructions. The style is flowing and elegant, usually portentous and elevated. The drawings are often filled with incredibly precise patterning and tiny details, and have an organic appearance similar to that of growing plants or crystals.

LIMITATIONS OF AUTOMATIC WRITING AND DRAWING

On the negative side, it has been observed by critics that automatic writings and drawings usually contain very little that is truly original or important. When produced by great artists, such automatic creations sometimes exhibit features of excellence. This was certainly true of the automatic drawings of the magician and artist Austin Osman Spare, and of the automatic poetry of the poet and artist William Blake. When done by individuals who show no artistic or literary talent in other areas of life, however, automatic writings and drawings are usually sterile exercises in technique. They look impressive at first glance, but lack artistic substance.

Unless you are already an artist, or have a strong, latent ability to write or draw, it is unlikely that your automatic writings or drawings will win you any prizes. On the other hand, automatic writing is an excellent way to receive scried information in an intelligible form. It is much more explicit in the meaning it conveys than the sometimes cryptic images we scry in the crystal or mirror, and a much easier way to receive messages than the pendulum or

Ouija board. Those scryers who can write automatically should consider themselves quite fortunate to possess this rare and useful talent.

CHAPTER 23

Automatic Speaking

AUTOMATIC SPEECH IS A FORM OF SCRYING

Automatic speaking is the audible exercise of the vocal cords independent of the conscious intention of the person who emits the sounds. It exhibits itself in the form of inarticulate grunts and noises, speaking in tongues (real or imaginary), trance singing, and articulate speech. When automatic speech is received during mediumistic trance, it is called phonetic automatism or trance speaking.

This class of involuntary vocalization is a specialized type of motor automatism in which the physical organs of speech (lungs, vocal cords, tongue, lips) are controlled by the agents of the deep mind, often (though not always) for the purpose of conveying information gathered in extrasensory ways to the conscious awareness. Because it is a communication from the unconscious to the conscious mind, it may be classified as scrying, as the term is used in this book.

Trance Speaking

Most of us are familiar with trance speaking, in which a psychic or medium enters a condition similar to the hypnotic state, and unconsciously speaks with an altered voice and personality. Usually the agent responsible for trance speaking identifies itself as a discarnate spirit or the soul of a human being who has died. The difference between the ordinary, waking mannerisms and personality of the medium, and those of the possessing spirit, can be striking.

The most common feature of trance speaking is a lowering of tone or roughening of the voice, which sometimes seems to come from deep inside the abdomen or chest rather than from the throat. In almost all cases the conscious awareness of the medium is displaced by the speaking intelligence, but in rare instances the medium is able to remain aware while speaking automatically, and can listen to and remember the words spoken.

Trance Speaking a Form of Possession

I can see no difference between trance speaking and demonic possession, apart from the intention and behavior displayed by the possessing spirits. During demonic possession, the spirit who takes control of the vocal apparatus of the incarnate host acts maliciously and seeks to inflict emotional or physical harm, either on the body of the host, or, by using the body of the host as its instrument, on other persons. It sometimes tries to maintain possession on a permanent basis by displacing the normal consciousness of the host entirely.

During trance speaking, the possessing spirit acts with a certain amount of discretion and displays concern over the physical and mental well-being of the host. The degree of control exerted by such spirits varies greatly from the limited ability to use the vocal apparatus of the host to complete control of all the motor functions of the body. Usually spirits who communicate through trance speaking seek to convey information that they perceive as useful or important to living human beings. They leave the host voluntarily, and only take possession of the speech function at the invitation of the host medium.

"WIZARDS THAT PEEP AND THAT MUTTER"

Automatic speaking is as old as human history, and probably much older. It is referred to in an oblique way many times in the Bible. Phonetic automatism is mentioned in the New Testament favorably (see Mark 16:17, Acts 19:6), where it is regarded as a gift of the Holy Spirit, and unfavorable in the Old Testament (see Isaiah 8:19, 29:4), where it is regarded as the deceit of familiar spirits. It is probable that the biblical prophets sometimes delivered their inspired ravings in the form of trance speaking.

When King Saul went to consult with the witch (more properly shaman or magician) of Endor, he sought to gain useful information from the utterances of the familiar spirit of the witch, who spoke through the vocal apparatus of the witch while the conscious awareness of the witch was displaced. Saul conversed with the ghost of the prophet Samuel, not face to face as you might be led to assume from the description in the Bible (see 1 Samuel 28:15-9) but through the witch, who acted as a medium.

VENTRILOQUISTS

The Romans called such spirit mediums ventriloquists, a word that means "one who speaks from the belly." Modern ventriloquism is nothing more than a contrived imitation of the real phenomenon of automatic speaking. The Greeks called their automatic speakers Eurycleis, after an Athenian scryer and medium named Eurycles, who was surnamed by his fellow citizens Engastromythes ("speech in the belly"). Eurycles must have been famous. His name became proverbial. The playwright Aristophanes mentions him in the play *The Wasps,* and Plato refers to him in a passage in his dialogue *The Sophist.*

The Greek writer Plutarch, who lived during the first century A.D., makes an interesting reference to this type of trance speaking, which appears to have been universally recognized as a genuine phenomenon throughout the ancient world:

> For it is a very childish and silly thing, to suppose that the god [Apollo] himself does, like the spirits speaking in the bowels of ventriloquists (which were anciently called Euryclees, and now Pythons), enter into the bodies of the prophets, and speak by their mouths and voices, as fit instruments for that purpose.[58]

The same type of automatic speech was observed by Traugott K. Oesterreich in his classic examination of possession. The details he describes are undoubtedly identical to those familiar to the ancient Greeks and Romans in connection with ventriloquists:

The second characteristic which reveals change of personality is closely related to the first: it is the voice. At the moment when the countenance alters, a more or less changed voice issues from the mouth of the person in the fit. The intonation also corresponds to the character of the new individuality manifesting itself in the organism and is conditioned by it. In particular the top register of the voice is displaced; the feminine voice is transformed into a bass one, for in all the cases of possession which it has hitherto been my lot to know the new individuality was a man.[59]

FIRST EXPERIENCES WITH AUTOMATIC SPEECH

Some of those who speak automatically for the first time have an experience similar to that of automatic writers. Prior to the first exhibition of automatic writing, the unconscious seizes control of the writing arm and moves it vigorously, as if to burn in a pathway for future nerve impulses that will control the writing. In the early stages of automatic speaking, the head and jaw sometimes move spasmodically, and strange, guttural sounds are emitted from the throat, or words without significant meaning.

A journalist who attended a spiritualist camp meeting in 1894 went through this preliminary burning-in process, which he reported in the *Proceedings* of the Society for Psychical Research. He was fortunate enough to remain fully conscious throughout the experience, although he lost his voluntary motor control.

Without warning, and no doubt to his great consternation, he felt his head forced powerfully backward until he lay flat on the ground. His head and jaw began to jerk, and then, in his words: "My mouth made automatic movements, till in a few seconds I was distinctly conscious of another's voice—unearthly, awful, loud, weird—bursting through the woodland from my own lips, with the despairing words 'Oh, my people.' Mutterings of semi-purposive prophecy followed."[60]

SEIZED BY THE SPIRIT

This journalist, who chose to remain anonymous, was obviously not seeking such an experience consciously and felt acute embarrassment at having it thrust upon him. The same involuntary speech, usually accompanied by some form of involuntary possession, occurs so often at religious congregations of Southern Baptist snake-handlers, worshipers of Voudoun and kindred South American spiritist sects that it is scarcely worthy of notice. Frequently the speech of these involuntary scryers is guttural or slurred, probably because the necessary channels between the unconscious mind and the physical speech organs have not been fully opened.

At these charismatic religious gatherings, spirit possession in invited by the worshipers consciously. They aid in the induction of a suitable receptive state by employing rhythmic movements of the body, such as dancing or shaking, and rhythmic sounds, such as chanting and drumming. Possession by spirits, or in Christian groups by the Holy Spirit, is the prime object, but automatic speaking is frequently produced, often in the form known as speaking in tongues.

SPEAKING IN TONGUES

Speaking in tongues, or languages other than the native language, is technically know as xenoglossis. When the words spoken do not correspond to any known language, the term glossolalia is sometimes used. The kind of unintelligible, pseudo-language that pours forth off the tongues of Christian Fundamentalists when they are seized by the Spirit would be classified as glossolalia.

Frequently it is asserted by spirits that this torrent of meaningless sound is actually the language of the angels, which they used before the expulsion of Adam and Eve from the Garden of Eden. The Enochian language received by Dr. John Dee and his seer, the alchemist Edward Kelley, is an example of the tongue of angels. Regarding the angelic tongue, the mystic and seer Emanuel Swedenborg (1688-1772) wrote:

> There is a universal language, proper to all angels and spirits, which has nothing in common with any language spoken in the world. Every man, after death, uses this language, for it is implanted in every one from creation; and therefore throughout the whole spiritual world all can understand one another. I have frequently heard this language and, having compared it with languages in the world, have found that it has not the slightest resemblance to any of them; it differs from them in this fundamental respect, that every letter of every word has a particular meaning.[61]

If there really is such a proto-language on some unknown plane of reality, it must be based on numerical relationships. Mathematics is the universal language of mankind. In this context, it is interesting to note the remark of the medium who preferred to be known as Mrs. H. concerning a scried language, which, as she asserted, "was natural to her and to all men." Her biographer, Justinus Kerner, writes concerning this universal language: "The written characters of this language were always connected with numbers. She said that words with numbers had a much deeper and more comprehensive significance than without."[62]

You may wonder how a language that has no correspondence with any language on Earth can be used to transmit information. Those who speak in tongues, either foreign languages they are not familiar with or apparent strings of meaningless syllables, sometimes see the meaning of the words appear written in their own language upon the air before their eyes even as they are in the act of uttering them. Sometimes they hear an internal translation of the words as they speak. This is known as the "interpretation of tongues."

SPEECH IN FOREIGN LANGUAGES

The evidence that any psychic has been able to speak fluently in an unfamiliar language is poor. Those who speak clearly and intelligibly are usually found to have learned the language as a child, or been exposed to it in childhood. More commonly, speaking in tongues consists of disconnected words and phrases in foreign languages that presumably were overheard and remembered unconsciously by the speaker.

Advantages and Disadvantages

The occurrence of automatic speech in the native language of the speaker is both more common and more useful as a medium of scrying. Its advantage is that it allows the agents of the deep mind to express many complex concepts and to convey a large volume of data quickly and clearly. Its disadvantage is that the speaker is usually (though not always) unconscious during the speaking session, and only learns what has been said after the session ends and others present repeat the words of the session.

Thanks to tape recorders and video recorders, it is possible in modern times for an automatic speaker to work alone by setting up a microphone to capture the words uttered during a scrying session, and then playing them back and analyzing them once the session ends and consciousness returns. However, the customary loss of awareness during automatic speaking makes this form of automatism generally less desirable than automatic writing, where consciousness is usually retained.

Not all psychics lose consciousness when their unconscious minds speak through them. Mrs. John H. Curran, who acted as the medium for the spirit that called itself Patience Worth, had complete control while the spirit was dictating its literary creations through Mrs. Curran's voice box. During the transmission of *Telka,* a 70,000-word poem in the Anglo-Saxon tongue, Mrs. Curran smoked cigarettes, got up to answer the telephone, and broke off the transmission from time to time to engage in casual conversation with those present.

CHANNELERS

In recent years the phenomenon of automatic speaking has received a renewed interest through the prophetic utterances of channelers, who act as the vehicle for various spirits. These spirits, who sometimes claim to be the souls of former inhabitants of Atlantis, ancient Egypt, or other exotic places, hold regular seminars during which they dispense personal advice or transmit teachings of a social or spiritual nature.

Channeling is just nineteenth century spiritualism under a new name. Channelers are spirit mediums, nothing more, nothing less. All of the phenomena that occur during channeling are well documented in the annals of the Society for Psychical Research.

In general, channelers dispense with the traditional ritual trappings that were sometimes employed by trance mediums during the Victorian Era. They merely sit comfortably and allow the communicating spirit, which fulfills the role of their spirit familiar, to take control of their vocal cords and speak through them. Usually they remain unconscious while the spirit has control and do not remember afterwards what they have spoken. Some channelers act as mediums for two or several spirits, but usually one spirit is dominant.

HOW TO ACHIEVE AUTOMATIC SPEECH

A good preparation for automatic speaking is to attain some degree of skill in other methods of scrying. These serve to establish a working link between your deep mind and conscious awareness. There is often a crossover between various forms of automatism. Many mediums begin using the pendulum or Ouija board, then progress to automatic writing or speaking. This was the case with Mrs. Curran, mentioned earlier, who began her communications with the spirit Patience Worth through the use of the Ouija, and progressed to automatic speech.

To encourage automatic speech directly, you can try visualization exercises designed to direct your unconscious mind into this channel of expression. Sit comfortably in a dimly lighted, quiet room. Close your eyes. Visualize your throat glowing with spiritual radiance. Imagine a warm and vibrating energy focused on your voice box in the form of a whirling vortex of light.

VOWEL VOCALIZATION

To facilitate this visualization, you should sound the vowels in succession, sustaining each for as long as you can comfortably hold it on a single breath. This is not an arbitrary exercise. The Gnostics and Hermetists of ancient Egypt used this vowel technique extensively in their magic and considered it to possess the highest occult power. The vowels are the living part of human speech. When sounded, they reverberate on the level of the unconscious mind.

Ideally, you will vibrate the vowels in your chest so that the sound fills your throat and issues forth with a deep, resonant tone. This technique requires that you sit upright, keep your throat open, and allow the sound to reflect off your diaphragm. If you are doing it properly, you will be able to feel the vibration when you place your hand upon your chest.

After you have gone through the sequence of the five English vowels a dozen times (French scryers would use the French vowels, German scryers the German vowels, etc.), begin to run the vowels together smoothly in a single breath, so that all five vowel sounds are expressed in each cycle: A-E-I-O-U. Do this a dozen times. Then return to the single vowel sounds.

THE CONVERSATION OF YOUR GUARDIAN ANGEL

This combined exercise of visualizing spiritual energy focused on the voice box, and at the same time sounding the vowel sounds with measured, rhythmic breaths, is very powerful and effective. When you have done this for fifteen or twenty minutes, relax your throat and mentally ask your guardian angel to speak to you through your own voice. This is best done within the sphere of light after you have mentally invoked your guardian, who is perceived to be standing behind your chair. Repeat your request clearly in your mind over and over for several minutes while you mentally project the words into the mind of your guardian.

Once you have clearly and repeatedly stated your desire, begin to hold a mental conversation with your guardian, just as though you are speaking out loud to a living person who stands behind your chair. Occasionally, pause in your internal monologue and allow your mind to fall completely silent. Indicate with an inner mental question mark that you would like your guardian to answer.

VALUE OF AUTOMATIC SPEECH AS A FORM OF SCRYING

I cannot guarantee that this exercise will result in automatic speech, which is a rare gift even among scryers. However, if you already possess the talent for automatic speaking latently within yourself, this exercise will help to develop it and bring it out. You should ask yourself if you really want this ability, which usually carries with it a loss of conscious control over the body, or even temporary unconsciousness of your surroundings during the period of speaking.

Trust is a laudable virtue. However, in my own work I have deliberately avoided those forms of scrying that result in a loss of conscious control over my body, or a loss of awareness of my actions and environment. My feeling is that, while most spirits may be trusted most of the time, it is only tempting fate to trust all spirits all of the time. You may decide, as I have, that the crystal, Ouija board, pendulum, and other physical scrying tools meet all your needs.

Chapter 24

Nature Scrying

"A World of Glass"

The earliest forms of scrying relied on natural phenomena and were conducted out-of-doors. Any sight or sound of nature with a mesmerizing or entrancing quality might be used to induce the receptive mental state needed for sensory automatism.

The forms given below are not arbitrary. Most, and perhaps all, of them were used in a formal ritual way by the priests and shamans of the ancient world to gather extrasensory information. Some have survived into modern culture as the playthings of children. This often happens with the techniques of magic. The casting of lots became dice. The Tarot devolved into ordinary playing cards used for gambling. The runes degenerated into a simple written script.

The different kinds of nature scrying have been divided under the two primary senses of seeing and hearing. There is often an overlap when two or more senses are engaged at once. For example, waterfall scrying relies on both sight and sound to produce a receptive mental state.

Scrying by Sight

WAVE SCRYING

If you have ever stood upon a dock or a boulder beside the water and stared down into the waves to watch them rhythmically rise and fall, you know just how hypnotic it can be. The motion of the water is particularly riveting if the sunlight or moonlight plays upon the crests. There is a strong sense of being drawn into the water, or of being pulled out of your own body.

Because of the obvious dangers this can pose, you should never attempt wave scrying unless you are seated or lying in a safe place where there is no risk of tumbling into the water. This is the practical warning of the myth of the sirens, beautiful water nymphs who lure sailors to their deaths with their entrancing songs. It is also the meaning behind the tales of Undines living in rivers and lakes who seduce men and pull them under the surface to their deaths.

Water has always been recognized to exert an almost overpowering attraction upon the minds of those who by their inherent nature are receptive to its influence. There is a subliminal sexuality in this attraction. Many of those who commit suicide by drowning fall prey to this fascination. When a scryer captures a small amount of water in a basin and brings it under a roof to scry into, this power is in some measure controlled; but when water scrying is conducted outdoors in natural bodies of water there is some danger that this seductive allure can race unchecked. Those over whom the water exerts too powerful a sway should confine themselves to scrying in the basin.

SMOKE SCRYING

This is a type of fire scrying, but deserves to be mentioned here because in ancient times fires for cooking and heating were often made out-of-doors under the open sky. Hunters or travelers spent many hours sitting before camp fires, often just before settling themselves down to sleep. In the still of twilight when the wind dies and the birds fall silent, the rising billows of wood smoke provide a potent medium for scrying visions, and the crackle of the wood seems almost to speak.

Smoke scrying is done by sitting or lying comfortably in visual range of the campfire and watching the smoke rise past your field of view. Do not attempt to follow it upward with your eyes. Merely allow it to paint a moving, swirling tapestry. Allow your awareness to pass into this rising curtain and through it. You may be rewarded by visions of distant lands and far-off times.

A special type of smoke scrying is that practiced by the American Indians. It is called a sweat lodge. Heated rocks are placed upon a hearth within a closed tent and water is poured over them to create steam. This is not scried visually but inhaled by those who sit naked within the tent seeking prophetic visions. The high temperature and humidity, coupled with the elevated levels of carbon dioxide, produce an intoxicated state in which detailed visions can arise.

The sweat lodge can be dangerous and should never be attempted except under the guidance of an experienced shaman. Nor should this ordeal be undertaken alone. It is necessary to have watchful friends nearby who can remove you from the lodge if you fall into unconsciousness.

CLOUD SCRYING

As most children have discovered, lying upon the grass and watching clouds pass overhead can induce a dreaming, receptive state that is ideal for visions. One person may see an image in the clouds, and be quite disappointed when others lying nearby cannot see it. This occurs because the first person has unconsciously scried the image, which is merely suggested by the pattern of the cloud, not actually delineated by it. To the individual who sees it, the image looks perfectly distinct, and the scryer cannot understand why everyone else has difficulty making it out.

It may happen that a single image in the clouds is shared between several or many observers. Frequently in history symbols or scenes of religious or political importance have been scried by groups. When the Emperor Constantine was marching against the army of Maxentius at Rome in 312, he and his entire army saw a shining cross of light amid the clouds of a noontime sky. One writer states that the cross contained the Greek words "By this conquer." That night Christ appeared to Constantine in a dream bearing a cross in his hand and ordered the Emperor to have a military standard made in the same image. Under this standard his badly outnumbered army was victorious against Maxentius.

Aerial armies are frequently sighted at times of great political uncertainty, and entire military battles have been witnessed in the clouds. Herne the Hunter is sometimes seen riding across the sky with his hounds, and the warriors of Woden are observed and heard flying abroad in the heavens. Some of the unidentified flying objects sighted in modern times have been shown to be curious disk-shaped cloud formations. While these do not look much like flying saucers in themselves, they may be perceived this way by someone who has achieved a receptive mental state through unconscious cloud scrying. The enthusiastic assertions of one person can act as inductive suggestions on others, and cause many gathered observers to scry a vision that was initially seen by only one cloud-gazer.

Cloud scrying only works under certain favorable conditions. The weather must be warm and pleasant, so that you can sit or lie outside for an hour or more. You must be alone or isolated in such a way that no other person is going to interrupt you by speaking or touching you. Cloud conditions must be good. A few small, independent clouds are not ideal for scrying. Neither is a dense overcast. The best conditions exist when the clouds are thick and move slowly across the sky, but are broken by patches of blue and strongly delineated by shadow and sunlight. White puffy clouds with some darkness of moisture in their bellies work well, especially if these grow and change while you watch them.

I find it best to lie down on the grass or upon the sun-warmed surface of a large rock. This puts the clouds directly before me eyes and frees me from any exertion. Do not become fixated on any particular cloud formation. Allow the clouds to drift across your passive field of view, and permit your attention to go where it wants to go. Simply watch the clouds without expectation. Visions cannot be forced. They must always be allowed to rise on their own.

Scrying by Sound

SHELL-HEARING

This is the most popular modern method for inducing clairaudience, the perception of sounds and voices received by extrasensory means. Everyone is familiar with the sound that can be heard when a large seashell is held up over the ear. It is a rushing, pulsing noise that resembles the sound of ocean waves breaking softly on a sandy beach. In reality, the wave noise is caused by the reflection of the tiny sounds of blood flowing through the vessels in your ear and the side of your head, as well as any ambient noise that may be in the air around you.

If you listen to this rushing pulse, and allow it to lull your mind into a receptive state, soon you will begin to make out fragments of distant conversation. This comes as if borne on the wind from some neighboring garden party. You will not be able to make out actual words at first, or no more than the occasional word or two. Eventually you will come to distinguish whole segments of conversation. The subjects of the talk will be quite meaningless and innocuous at the early stages.

As this ghostly garden party becomes clearer, mentally try to break into the conversation. If you are fortunate and have an innate skill for this type of scrying, you may find that one or more of the voices will respond to your mental comments and engage you in conversation, just as though you were standing with them at the party with a glass in your hand.

Shell-hearing is the easiest form of clairaudience from which to gain frequent, consistent results. This

may be because the sound audible in the shell is so
close to the sound of distant human conversation, even
without any scrying ability. This background shell
noise is always consistent, and is instantly available
to you each time you raise the shell to your ear.

You will want to find a large, attractive shell with
an opening that you can easily and comfortably hold
to your ear. These can often be located in craft and
gift stores. If you are fortunate enough to live close to
the ocean, you may be able to find your shell on the
beach. Experiment with different shells until you
locate one that feels comfortable in the hand and produces a strong, pleasing sound.

When using it, hold it to your left ear if you are
right-handed, unless you are partially deaf in the left
ear. Always hold the shell to whichever ear hears
most clearly. If both ears are of the same acuteness,
left-handed persons should hold the shell to their
right ears. The left side is receptive in right-handed
individuals; the right side is usually receptive in
those who are left-handed. Experiment with both
ears to discover which side works best for you.

WATERFALL SCRYING

This class of techniques involves audio-scrying with
the sound of running or falling water. It was used by
the ancient Greek priests who presided over the
shrines built around sacred springs and fountains.
Water falling from a height or rushing rapidly over
irregular rocks produces a sound that is similar to the
distant murmur of many voices. By listening for prolonged periods to this sound, it is possible to induce a
receptive scrying state in which individual articulate

voices begin to emerge from the general background noise of the water.

Sacred springs, where the water bubbled up from the ground with a steady flow at all times of the year, were worshiped as the habitation of nymphs—female spirits who like to interact with human beings, and sometimes give those they favor the gifts of wisdom and prophecy. It was not uncommon for kings or heroes to wed these water nymphs just as they would marry a mortal woman. This may have had a religio-social function. By linking the bloodline of the king with the local deity of a sacred spring, the descendants of that king assumed the status of demigods. It also fulfilled a more immediate and practical need of the hero to acquire occult power and wisdom.

One of the most famous of these marriages took place between Numa, the second king of Rome (reigned 716-673 B.C.), and the nymph Egeria. Each night the King would visit his spirit wife at her sacred spring, where she would teach him the system of laws which he later gave to all the Romans. The Roman historian Varro regarded this marriage as a metaphorical fable signifying that King Numa used the Persian method of divination by water called hydromancy to scry his sacred laws.

This skepticism arose from the decadence of religion that occurred under the Caesars, and is unwarranted in this instance. Very probably Numa went through a formal marriage ceremony with the nymph Egeria, who was represented by a symbolic statue or other vessel. He may well have consulted the oracle of her priests or priestesses on a regular basis, which would have occurred at the temple of the nymph built upon or near her sacred spring.

When a spring was deemed to be sacred, it was often enclosed with stone into a fountain or well. The temple of the deity believed to inhabit the spring was erected either directly over the spring, or very close by. It was common for sacred springs to give oracles to worshipers who came seeking guidance. These were ministered by the priests or priestesses of the deity, who relied upon the inquiries of visitors to the spring as a source of income.

In Christian times the pagan temples were torn down and churches erected upon their foundations. These churches enclosed the sacred springs, either within their walls or within their immediate grounds. Some of the nymphs became Christian saints. Many ancient churches of Europe have almost forgotten pagan sacred springs where these nymphs continue to dwell, asleep and dreaming, but ready to awaken when they are once more worshiped.

When you hear a voice speak from within a spring or waterfall, there is a good chance that you are hearing the voice of its resident nymph. It is prudent to offer hymns of praise and sacrifices of food, drink, or valuable objects such as coins to the water source if you wish the nymph to give you friendship and service. Visit the spring often. Converse with the nymph as though with a beloved companion. Maintain an attitude of respect toward her. In this way she may develop affection for you and help you.

WIND SCRYING

A demon of the Canadian Indians is the Wendigo. The Wendigo is a horrible cannibal fiend who dines on human flesh and rides the wind. Whenever the

Indians heard the wind roaring high overhead when all around them in the forest the air was breathlessly still, they used to say the Wendigo was passing.

Anyone who has experienced this strange phenomenon can understand why they were terrified. Under certain conditions the air at the level of the trees can be completely calm while at the same time the air higher in the atmosphere rushes past with the speed and noise of a locomotive. It is an eerie experience.

The wind lends itself naturally to clairaudient scrying because it sounds a great deal like a human voice even to average persons with no trace of psychic ability. By listening to it attentively it is possible to begin to distinguish words in a very short time. Usually you will not hear the voice of the wind in its pristine purity, as you do when the Wendigo passes. It is much more common to hear it through the sounds it makes in the grass, or in the leaves of trees, or at the chimney or eves of your house.

The ancient Greeks practiced wind scrying in the leaves of the oaks in the sacred grove of Dodona, which was dedicated to Zeus. Psellus was referring to this technique when he wrote "there is a mode of predicting by means of the air and the leaves of trees."[63] The precise method is uncertain, but it seems to have involved the hanging of striking wands from the branches of sacred oaks in such a way that they struck resounding brass basins when the wind blew. Interpretations were made of the sound of the wind in the leaves and of the striking brass.

The best way to scry the wind is to sit close to a tree that creates a large volume of sound when the wind blows through its branches. If you listen attentively, you may be able to pick out the voice of the tree spirit and distinguish its words. It used to be said that the wind carried voices within it from distant places. These psychic voices become caught, as it were, in the boughs of trees, where you can hear them if you listen for them.

Another excellent way to scry the wind is with a chimney. Sit beside the fireplace and listen to the voice that moans and sighs down the flue on windy nights. Allow it to talk to you and tell you its secrets. The more human the wind sounds, the greater the likelihood that you will eventually be able to distinguish its hidden words if you listen long enough.

You can talk back to the wind if you wish. For centuries sailors have "whistled up the wind" when caught in a prolonged calm. It is also possible to whistle down the wind when it is blowing too fiercely. I developed this technique in childhood and have used it for many years. It is quite effective at providing a local calm where the wind does not blow, even when the wind is still raging only a few hundred feet away.

Focus your awareness on the howling of the wind. Put the tip of your tongue behind your teeth close to your upper gum and make a very breathy hissing or hushing sound through your parted lips, the same sound you would make when trying to quiet a noisy or unruly child. Gradually reduce the strength of this sound while at the same time mentally reaching out with your mind to soothe the wind. Allow the hushing sound to fade down into silence while still exhaling very softly and concentrate strongly on stillness while holding the sound of the wind in your mind.

If you do this properly, you will find that you can "hush" the wind even when it is blowing with gale force. You will hear it still howling not far away, but it will cease to blow around your house or the immediate area where you are standing for up to a minute before it begins to strengthen again. If the gusts are strong and rapid, you may have to repeat this hushing quite often to maintain a calm.

Skeptics would argue that whistling the wind up or down is only self-deception. If you wait long enough, the wind will always gain or lessen in strength. This may be true. However, the subjective effect of soothing the wind is to establish a living union between your consciousness and the wild dreaming mind of nature. In order to whistle down the wind you must, for a time, become the wind. When you do so, the sense of controlling the wind is very strong and real.

CHAPTER 25

Dream Scrying

SCRYED VERSUS PROPHETIC DREAMS

Dream scrying is the deliberate effort to cause an oracular or revelatory dream that will answer a specific question. Prophetic dreams that occur spontaneously as warnings or foreshadowings of future events cannot be considered dream scrying because they have not been consciously sought. The question may be very specific ("Where did my departed uncle bury his money?") or more general ("What must I do to succeed in this present business venture?"). The dream response may be given indirectly in the form of symbolic visions that must be interpreted, or directly as a clear, specific image or audible speech.

GREEK DREAM TEMPLES

As is true of most of the scrying methods in this book, dream scrying is very old. Its origins are lost in time, but it was frequently employed by the ancient Egyptians and Greeks. The Greeks commonly sought dream oracles within the sacred space of a temple, and relied upon the formal methods used by the priests. Certain temples were famous throughout the ancient world as dream oracles.

Among these might be noted the temple of Amphiaraus at Oropos, an ancient Greek town that was located at present-day Skala Oropou, not far from Kalamos. There was a white statue of the god inside a temple near a sacred spring. The Greek geographer Pausanias (second century A.D.) says that Amphiaraus was particularly noted as a giver of dreams, and was "recognized as a god for having instituted oracular dreaming." The procedure was to go to the temple and purify oneself by making offerings to the gods on the altar of the temple, then to sacrifice a ram, remove its fleece and use it as a sleeping mat inside the temple.

Cicero makes mention of the temple of Pasiphae, which was located in the countryside not far from Sparta. The magistrates of the city used to go to this temple and spend the night there in order to receive dream answers to difficult questions "because they considered the oracles received in sleep to be true." Pasiphae was the daughter of the solar god Helios.

Another god closely connected with dream scrying is Serapis, because this god first made his existence known to Ptolemy Soter of Egypt (367-283 B.C.) through an oracular dream. There were forty-two temples of Serapis in Egypt during the time of the Ptolemys, and many more in other lands. Cicero mentions this god along with the Greek god of healing, Aesculapius, as givers of dream oracles. Dream scrying was frequently used to discover the best remedy for an illness, and for this reason is often connected with healing gods and goddesses.

ST. PATRICK'S PURGATORY

The practice of sleeping in religious shrines for the purpose of receiving an oracular dream continued into Christian times. The most famous dream shrine was the cave known as St. Patrick's Purgatory, located on an island in Lough Derg in Donegal, Ireland. The faithful would entomb themselves in six tiny cells for nine days, living only on bread and water and leaving the cells only to pray, and wait for a vision of what awaited them in hell. As strange as it sounds, this dream oracle was enormously popular.

THEOPEMPTOI

Oracular dreams were known as *theopemptoi* ("sent from God"). Writing about them, Iamblichus says:

> ...they take place either when sleep is leaving us, and we are beginning to awake, and then we hear a certain voice, which concisely tells us what is to be done; or voices are heard by us, between sleeping and waking, or when we are perfectly awake. And sometimes, indeed, an invisible and incorporeal spirit surrounds the recumbents, so as not to be perceived by the sight, but by a certain other cosensation and intelligence. The entrance of this spirit, also, is accompanied by a noise, and he diffuses himself on all sides without any contact, and effects admirable works conducive to the liberation of the passions of the soul and body. But sometimes a bright and tranquil light shines forth, by which the sight of the eyes is detained, and which occasions them to become closed, though they were before open. The other senses, however, are in a vigilant state,

and in a certain respect have a cosensation of the light
unfolded by the Gods; and the recumbents hear what
the Gods say, and know, by a consecutive perception,
what is then done by them. This, however, is beheld in
a still more perfect manner, when the sight perceives,
when intellect, being corroborated, follows what is performed, and this is accompanied with the motion of the
spectators.[64]

HYPNAGOGIC IMAGES

The emphasis laid by Iamblichus upon dreams that
occur just after we awaken is interesting because it is
at these times that we are most prone to experience
hypnagogic images. These are images seen, either
with the eyes closed or open, when we are half-asleep
and half-awake. They occur most commonly to children under the age of twelve years (the reason young
children were used as scryers by Egyptian and Babylonian magicians).

Hypnagogic images are quite clear, and may persist for up to a minute or two with the consciousness
turned directly upon them. Sometimes they are said
by those who see them to be quite small, no larger
than a snapshot or a postage stamp, but unnaturally
bright. Any attempt to manipulate the contents of
these images by the will usually banishes them. The
most common content of the images is distorted or
grotesque faces. D. H. Rawcliffe speculates that hypnagogic images may be responsible for the common
medieval representations of demons and gargoyles
that occur in Church art.[65]

If hypnagogic images are the source of some oracular dreams, this does not invalidate such dreams.

The same psychological mechanism may be at work in both cases, but hypnagogic images arise spontaneously and are undirected, whereas scried oracular dreams are deliberately sought by an act of will and concern specific events. The difference is the same that exists between random doodling and writing.

THE INSTRUCTIONS OF CORNELIUS AGRIPPA

About the method used by the Greeks, Cornelius Agrippa writes: "Hence it was a custom amongst the ancients, that they who should receive answers, certain sacred expiations and sacrifices being first celebrated, and divine worship ended, did religiously lie down even in a consecrated chamber, or at least on the skins of the sacrifices."[66]

We are fortunate to have many details of the methods used by the ancients for dream scrying. These will enable us to reconstruct a workable technique for modern scryers which does not entail the sacrifice of animals or sleeping within the walls of a sacred temple. First, let us examine the general instructions given by Agrippa to achieve an oracular dream:

> Therefore whosoever would receive divine dreams, let him be well disposed in body, his brain free from vapours, and his mind from perturbations, and let him that day abstain from supper, neither let him drink that which will inebriate, let him have a clean and neat chamber, also exorcised and consecrated: in the which, a perfume being made, his temples anointed, things causing dreams being put on his fingers, and the representation of the heavens being put under his

head, and paper being consecrated, his prayers being said, let him go to bed, earnestly meditating on that thing he desireth to know: so he shall see most true and certain dreams with the true illumination of his intellect.[67]

A CLEAR GLASS FOR PROPHESYING

It is necessary to have a calm, peaceful state of both mind and body. Never attempt to dream scry when you are sick or in pain or completely exhausted. Nor should you scry when your brain is overheated by some mental labor, or you are very worried, or frightened, or angry. Elsewhere Agrippa writes: "Therefore it is necessary, that he who would receive true dreams, should keep a pure, undisturbed, and an undisquieted imaginative spirit ... for such a spirit is most fit for prophesying, and (as Sinesius saith) is a most clear glass of all the images which flow everywhere from all things."[68]

The reason hypnagogic images are so often frightening or grotesque is because the mind receiving them is in an unquiet state. As is true of a lake disturbed by the wind, it cannot reflect a true image. This is the reason Agrippa lays stress on the importance of a moderate diet, and the omission of an evening meal on the night of dream scrying. It is well known that eating just before bed can induce nightmares. All forms of scrying and spirit communication are aided by moderate fasting. Remember, those Christians who visited the cave of St. Patrick ate only bread and water for eight days, and on the ninth day they ate nothing at all.

ONE DAY FROM FOOD,
THREE DAYS FROM WINE

Alcohol and drugs of any kind will completely destroy
your chance of receiving an oracular dream. You may
well have hallucinations after drinking liquor or
smoking pot, but what you see will not be sent by the
gods. Philostratus wrote that Amphiaraus, a prophet
who gave oracles in Attica, counseled those who
sought dream oracles to abstain one entire day from
food, and three full days from wine "in order that he
may imbibe the oracles with his soul in a condition of
utter transparency."[69]

CLEANLINESS IS NEXT TO GODLINESS

The room in which you sleep must be scrupulously
clean because anything disordered or soiled is repugnant to the heavenly gods and angels. The same is
true of your own body. For this reason it is a good
practice to shower or bathe just before seeking a
dream oracle, and to recite the cleansing prayer
already given in the chapter on ritual. Your pajamas
or other sleeping garments should also be perfectly
clean, as should your sheets, pillowcase and blankets.
This may seem like an unnecessary precaution, but
the Greeks, Egyptians, Hebrews, and indeed all cultures of the ancient world stress the need for absolute
cleanliness in dealing with the gods.

"THINGS CAUSING DREAMS"

The "things causing dreams" that Agrippa says
should be placed on the fingers are probably magic

rings inscribed to the god or gods presiding over dream oracles, and having dream-producing herbs under their stones. The "perfume" is an appropriate incense. Clean oil is used to anoint the temples of the head to sanctify them. Dreams were believed to enter through the head. For the same reason, Agrippa counsels that a "representation of the heavens" be placed under the pillow. It should be drawn on consecrated paper, and perhaps contains the astrological chart for the night the dream oracle is sought.

Prayers are very important, and should not be omitted. The reason prayers are so often said just prior to going to sleep is because they are believed in this way to go directly to the ears of God. In pagan times prayers were recited seven times over to the god of oracular dreams. This might be Serapis, or Amphiaraus, or Pasiphae, or Aesculapius or the Egyptian god Bes, or some other deity strongly connected with dream oracles.

THE MAGICAL PAPYRI

The actual method used by Egyptian magicians to procure prophetic dreams has been preserved in the spells contained in the Greek magical papyri, which were written down from 200 B.C. to A.D. 500. Most of these are in an incomplete form and contain numerous breaks in the text and corruptions, but it is possible to use these magical texts to construct a general ritual for dream scrying that may be worked by modern scryers.

Egyptian Ritual for Dream Scrying

PREPARATION AND SETTING

It is important that you do not speak to anyone on the evening of the scrying. Absolute silence should be maintained after the setting of the Sun. Do not eat anything for at least six hours before the dream scrying, and do not drink any alcohol. Do not engage in sex on the day of the ritual.

The ritual is performed at night in the bedroom just before getting into bed. After bathing and reciting the prayer of personal cleansing given earlier in this book, anoint your temples with drops of pure olive oil. Rub the oil into your temples with the tips of your index fingers using a circular motion until you feel a mild warmth. Also put a drop upon your third eye, between your eyebrows.

INSTRUMENTS

The key instrument for dream scrying is what was called the "day lamp," presumably the common or everyday oil lamp used by Egyptians to light their houses. The only condition specified is that the lamp must not be colored red and must not bear any inscription. Upon a short, narrow strip of clean, white linen the dream scryer writes with myrrh ink (ink mixed with myrrh) the name of the dream god and the purpose for the dream scrying. This linen strip is then twisted into a wick and inserted into the oil of the lamp. The type of oil used varies, but sesame oil and cedar oil are mentioned. You may use pure olive oil. Set the lamp on a table beside your bed. Put it in the eastern side of the bedroom, if possible.

Using the same ink you used to write down the purpose of the scrying and the name of the dream god on the linen wick, draw the image of the god upon your left palm. Since myrrh ink is fairly hard to come by these days, you may use a magic marker with dark blue, purple, or black ink for both wick and palm, if you must. A better alternative is to put a drop of scented oil in black artist's ink. Use a scent extract that is very heavy and sweet, and has a mild narcotic effect. Use myrrh, if you can find it.

THE DREAM GOD

You must decide before beginning which god or goddess you will rely on to send you true dreams. The ibis-headed god Thoth was very popular with the Egyptians. He will be used in this example. Draw the outline of the god upon your left palm. This may be no more than a stick figure provided you know what the god actually looks like. You should study the images of Thoth in Egyptian art. Choose the image that shows the god as a standing human figure with the head of an ibis in profile, holding in his hands a reed pen and writing tablet.

Alternatively, you may draw the image of the god upon a clean sheet of paper. It is also useful to write the reason for conducting the dream scrying on the paper under the image of the god, using the same words you wrote upon the wick.

THE METHOD

Light the lamp. Kneel before it and by its light regard the image of the god upon your left palm (or upon the paper). Recite the following opening invocation. The Egyptians used various specific invocations to Thoth and other dream gods, but the general invocation given in the hymns of Orpheus is more flexible, should you choose to invoke other gods such as Isis or Apollo. In place of the word "Thee" in the first line of the following extract from the hymn, substitute the name of your dream god:

> Thee I invoke, blessed power of dreams divine,
> Angel of future fates, swift wings are thine;
> Great source of oracles to human kind,
> When stealing soft, and whispering to the mind,
> Through sleep's sweet silence and the gloom of night,
> Thy power awake the intellectual sight;
> To silent souls the will of heaven relates,
> And silently reveals their future fates.[70]

Next you need to concentrate strongly on the question you wish to have answered by your dream oracle. The following formula must be recited seven times in succession with total concentration on the question so that your breath touches and moves softly the flame of the lamp. Below I have given a formula of Thoth, but if you are using another god as your dream god, you must compose an appropriate formula which details the nature and powers of that god:

> Come to me, Thoth, mighty son of the Goddess who gifts with mental vision. Come to me, Blessed One, who sends forth oracles by day and night. Come to me quickly, you who are powerful in magic. Come to me, Lord of Truth, who loves truth, who knows truth, who judges truth, who does truth! I call upon you, appointed

god of gods over the spirits of the Earth, to show [insert here the subject of your dream inquiry] truly to me in dreams. I conjure you, great Thoth, by your father, Osiris; I conjure you, wise Thoth, by your mother, Isis; show yourself to me during sleep and reveal to me [insert here the subject of your dream inquiry] about which I inquire. Reveal everything I seek truly and without falsehood. Iao, Sabaoth, Adonai, Abrasax! Let it be done!

This formula is composed of parts of several actual Egyptian dream oracle incantations to Thoth. It is not necessary to memorize and recite the words exactly, provided you know why you are chanting it. The formula defines the powers of the dream god, informs the dream god what it is you wish to learn, and compels the dream god to obey you by the authority of the names of gods that rule over the dream god, and the use of barbarous names of invocation.

After you chant this (or a similar) formula seven times into the flame of the lamp, wrap a length of black linen that is about three inches wide and about thirty inches long around the image of the god that is drawn upon your left palm. Tuck the end in so that it does not unravel. If you have drawn the image on paper, wrap the black linen strip around the paper so that the paper is completely enfolded in the cloth and place the cloth beneath your pillow. This black cloth is called the "black" of Isis, and represents a strip from the hem of the black linen robe used by the priestesses of the Isis cult.

Blow out the flame of the lamp with your breath using your linen-wrapped left hand to cup the flame, and immediately get into your bed and go to sleep. Do not worry any further about the subject of the dream oracle. If you have performed the ritual properly, it will be imprinted upon your subconscious mind.

"A Certain Voice"

Have a pen and writing tablet beside your bed. If you awaken in the night, record any dreams you remember. If you sleep soundly all through the night, record any dreams you remember in the morning. You may hear a voice speaking to you. This will speak quite clearly and distinctly. It may be the voice of someone you know, or a voice completely strange. This is a direct response to your inquiry and is of the highest value. Record the words exactly as they are given as soon as you are able. Do not assume that you will remember them when you wake up in the morning.

I have received several of these direct dream oracles. They are always spoken in a clear voice. Usually, there is no dream image associated with them, although you may be dreaming of something else when you hear the voice of the god, which seems to come out of the air. The words are brief and sometimes cryptic. They must be studied upon awakening to extract meaning from them. The direct speech of the dream god is the most important form of dream oracle and should never be treated lightly.

You may repeat this dream scrying up to seven nights in succession using the same wick in the lamp and the same image upon your left palm (or on the paper under your pillow). If necessary, retrace the image of the god upon your palm each night before the lamp so that it remains sharply drawn while you sleep. During the days, place the lamp, the ink, and the black of Isis in a secure, dark place where they will not be disturbed, and never allow the sunlight to shine upon them.

Notes

1. Melville, John. *Crystal Gazing and Clairvoyance* (1896). Reprinted by Samuel Weiser, New York, 1970, p.78.

2. Apuleius, Lucius. *The Golden Ass* (2nd century). See Chapter 47.

3. *Marvels of the World.* In *The Book of Secrets of Albertus Magnus.* Best and Brightman, eds. Oxford University Press, London, 1974, p. 74.

4. *The Secret of the Golden Flower.* Richard Wilhelm, trans. (1931). Routledge & Kegan Paul, London,1962, p. 22.

5. Ward, Charles A. *Oracles of Nostradamus* (1891). Reprinted by The Modern Library (Random House), New York, 1940, p. 52.

6. Ibid., p. 54.

7. Ibid., p. 42.

8. Ibid., p. 44.

9. Ibid.

10. Ibid., pp. 68-69.

11. Iamblichus. *On the Mysteries of the Egyptians, Chaldeans, and Assyrians.* Translated from the Greek by Thomas Taylor (1821). Stuart & Watkins, London, 1968, pp. 143-144.

12. Psello, Michaele. *De daemonibus.* Quoted by Ward, *Oracles of Nostradamus,* pp. 75-76.

13. Marcellinus, Ammianus. *Rerum Gestarum.* Quoted by Ward, *Oracles of Nostradamus,* p. 77.

14. Samuel Daiches, *Babylonian Oil Magic* (1913). Reprinted in *Three Works of Ancient Jewish Magic,* Chthonios Books, 1986, Part 3, pp. 15-16.

15. Ibid., pp. 18-19.

16. Ibid., p. 5.

17. See *The Greek Magical Papyri in Translation.* Hans Dieter Betz, ed. University of Chicago Press, 1992, p. 42.

18. Griffith and Thompson, eds. *The Demotic Magical Papyrus of London and Leiden* (1904). Reprinted under the title *The Leyden Papyrus* by Dover Publications, New York, 1974, p. 35.

19. Ibid., pp. 27-29.

20. Ibid., p. 25.

21. Ibid., p. 31.

22. Homer. *The Odyssey.* See Book XI.

23. Halliwell, James Orchard, ed. *The Private Diary of Dr. John Dee.* Camden Society, London, 1842, pp. 11-12.

24. Ibid., p. 11.

25. Ashmole, Elias. *Theatrum Chemicum Britannicum.* London, 1652, p. 481.

26. For an account of Dee's scrying instruments, see Geoffrey James' *The Enochian Magick of Dr. John Dee,* Llewellyn Publications, St. Paul, 1995, Chapter 3.

27. See Adam McLean, *A Treatise on Angel Magic.* Phanes Press, Grand Rapids, MI, 1990, pp. 30-31. This work is the first publication of Harley MS 6482.

28. Spenser, Edmund. *The Faerie Queene,* Book III, Canto 2, Stanza 19.

29. Freer, Miss Goodrich. *Essays in Psychical Research.* Described by Nandor Fodor in *Encyclopaedia of the Occult* (1934). Reprinted by University Books, 1966, p. 73.

30. *Crystal Gazing and Clairvoyance,* p. 31.

31. George Laurence Gomme, *The Gentleman's Magazine Library: Popular Superstitions,* Elliot Stock, London, 1884, pp. 59-60.

32. Ibid., p. 61.

33. *Marvels of the World,* Section 53. In *The Book of Secrets of Albertus Magnus,* p. 98.

34. *Rerum Gestarum,* 29, 1. Quoted by Ward, *Oracles of Nostradamus,* p. 77.

35. *Encyclopaedia of Psychic Science,* p. 270.

36. Ibid.

37. Ibid.

38. Blavatsky, Helena Petrovna. *Isis Unveiled* (1877). The Theosophy Company, Los Angeles, 1931, Vol. II, p. 95.

39. Quoted by Lewis Spence, *An Encyclopaedia of Occultism* (1920). Reprinted by University Books, New York, 1960, p. 51. Spence does not give his source.

40. Besant, Annie and C. W. Leadbeater. *Thought-Forms* (1901). Reprinted by Theosophical Publishing House, Wheaton, Ill. (abridged edition), p. 22.

41. Ibid., p. 43.

42. Quoted by Fodor, *Encyclopaedia of Psychic Science,* p. 39. Fodor does not give his source.

43. *Proceedings* S.P.R., Vol. X, p. 332. Quoted by Fodor, p. 320.

44. Mead, G. R. S. *Did Jesus Live 100 B.C.?* Quoted by Fodor, p. 319.

45. D'Aute-Hooper. *Spirit Psychometry.* Quoted by Fodor, p. 318.

46. *Encyclopaedia of Psychic Science,* page 319.

47. *Popular Superstitions,* p. 152.

48. Quoted by Spence, *An Encyclopaedia of Occultism,* p. 128.

49. *Popular Superstitions,* p. 317.

50. Ibid., p. 151.

51. *Encyclopaedia of Psychic Science,* p. 98.

52. Ibid.

53. Ibid.

54. Quoted by Fodor, *Encyclopaedia of Psychic Science,* p. 99.

55. Ibid., p. 19.

56. Ibid., p. 22.

57. Ibid., p. 23.

58. Plutarch. *The Obsolescence of Oracles,* Sec. 9.
In *Plutarch's Essays and Miscellanies* (1684-94),
William W. Goodwin, ed. (5 volumes), vol. 4, p. 13.

59. Osterreich, Traugott K. *Possession: Demonical
& Other* (1921). Reprinted by Causeway Books,
New York, 1974 under the title *Possession and
Exorcism,* pp. 19-20.

60. *Proceedings,* Vol. XII, pp. 277-98. Quoted by
Fodor, *Encyclopaedia of Psychic Science,* p. 25.

61. Swedenborg, Emanuel. *The True Christian Religion.* Quoted by Fodor, *Encyclopaedia of Psychic
Science,* p. 412.

62. Kerner, Justinus. *The Seeress of Provorst.* Quoted
by Fodor, *Encyclopaedia of Psychic Science,* p. 413.

63. Quoted by Charles A. Ward, *Oracles of
Nostradamus,* pp. 75-76.

64. *On the Mysteries,* pp. 115-116.

65. Rawcliffe, D. H. *The Psychology of the Occult.*
Dover, New York, 1959, p. 125.

66. Agrippa, Cornelius. *Three Books of Occult Philosophy* (1533). Annotated edition (Donald Tyson, ed.) reprinted by Llewellyn Publications, St. Paul, MN, 1993, p. 634.

67. Ibid., p. 635.

68. Ibid., p. 633.

69. Philostratus. *Life of Apollonius of Tyana.* F. C. Conybeare, trans. Harvard U. Press, 1912, Vol. I, p. 215.

70. *Hymns of Orpheus,* Thomas Taylor, trans. In *Thomas Taylor the Platonist: Selected Writings,* K. Raine and G. Mills Harper, eds. Princeton U. Press, Princeton, NJ, p. 290.

Divination For Beginners

Discover the Techniques that Work for You

Scott Cunningham

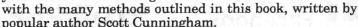

There's no need to visit a sooth-
sayer or call a psychic hotline
to glimpse into your future or to
uncover your past. You can become
your own diviner of things unseen
with the many methods outlined in this book, written by
popular author Scott Cunningham.

Here you will find detailed descriptions of both common
and unusual divinatory techniques, each grouped by the
tools or techniques used to perform them. Many utilize
natural forces such as water, clouds, smoke, and the movement of birds. Also discussed are the more advanced techniques of Tarot, Palmistry, and the I Ching.

0-7387-0384-2
264 pp., 5³⁄₁₆ x 8 $13.95

CHALDEAN NUMEROLOGY FOR BEGINNERS

How Your Name and Birthday Reveal Your True Nature & Life Path

Heather Alicia Lagan

Gain insight into your gifts and challenges with this simple and empowering divinatory system. Chaldean numerology paints a clear picture of you and your personal "blueprint"—your essence, talents, desires, lessons, and ideal direction for this lifetime. This introductory guide presents highly effective techniques for decoding the energetic vibrations and information held in names, birthdates, addresses, phone numbers, and much more.

Master numerologist Heather Alicia Lagan has simplified Chaldean numerology, making it both accessible and practical. She offers detailed sample readings of three celebrities—Apolo Anton Ohno, Leonardo DiCaprio, and Drew Barrymore—to help readers understand, share, and benefit from this treasury of ancient knowledge. Chaldean numerology, the original form of numerology upon which all later systems were based, offers guidance, inspirational and enlightening messages, and a framework for setting or achieving goals.

0-7387-2624-9

360 pp., 5³⁄₁₆ x 8 $15.95

A Practical Guide to the Runes

Their Uses in Divination and Magick

Lisa Peschel

At last the world has a beginner's book on the Nordic runes that is written in straightforward and clear language. Each of the twenty-five runes is elucidated through no-nonsense descriptions and clean graphics. A rune's altered meaning in relation to other runes and its reversed position is also included. The construction of runes and accessories covers such factors as the type of wood to be used, the size of the runes, and the coloration, carving, and charging of the runes. With this book the runes can be used in magick to effect desired results. Talismans carved with runescripts or bindrunes allow you to carry your magick in a tangible form, providing foci for your will. Four rune layouts complete with diagrams are presented with examples of specific questions to ask when consulting the runes. Rather than simple fortunetelling devices, the runes are oracular, empowered with the forces of Nature. They present information for you to make choices in your life.

0-87542-593-3
192 pp., 4 x 7 $6.99

DOWSING FOR BEGINNERS

How to Find Water, Wealth & Lost Objects

Richard Webster

This book provides everything you need to know to become a successful dowser. Dowsing is the process of using a dowsing rod or pendulum to divine for anything you wish to locate: water, oil, gold, ancient ruins, lost objects or even missing people. Dowsing can also be used to determine if something is safe to eat or drink, or to diagnose and treat allergies and diseases.

Learn about the tools you'll use: angle and divining rods, pendulums, wands—even your own hands and body can be used as dowsing tools! Explore basic and advanced dowsing techniques, beginning with methods for dowsing the terrain for water. Find how to dowse anywhere in the world without leaving your living room, with the technique of map dowsing. Discover the secrets of dowsing to determine optimum planting locations; to monitor your pets' health and well-being; to detect harmful radiation in your environment; to diagnose disease; to determine psychic potential; to locate archeological remains; to gain insight into yourself, and more! *Dowsing for Beginners* is a complete "how-to-do-it" guide to learning an invaluable skill.

1-56718-802-8
240 pp., 5³⁄₁₆ x 8 $13.95

PSYCHIC DEVELOPMENT FOR BEGINNERS

An Easy Guide to Releasing and Developing Your Psychic Abilities

William Hewitt

Psychic Development for Beginners provides detailed instruction on developing your sixth sense, or psychic ability. Improve your sense of worth, your sense of responsibility and therefore your ability to make a difference in the world. Innovative exercises like "The Skyscraper" allow beginning students of psychic development to quickly realize personal and material gain through their own natural talent.

Benefits range from the practical to spiritual. Find a parking space anywhere, handle a difficult salesperson, choose a compatible partner, and even access different time periods! Practice psychic healing on pets or humans—and be pleasantly surprised by your results. Use psychic commands to prevent dozing while driving. Preview out-of-body travel, cosmic consciousness and other alternative realities. Instruction in *Psychic Development for Beginners* is supported by personal anecdotes, 44 psychic development exercises, and 28 related psychic case studies to help students gain a comprehensive understanding of the psychic realm.

1-56718-360-3
216 pp., 5³⁄₁₆ x 8 $12.95

ASTRAL TRAVEL FOR BEGINNERS

Transcend Time and Space with Out-of-Body Experiences

Richard Webster

What you've done thousands of times in your sleep can now become a totally conscious experience with the help of this handy guidebook. You'll soon learn to leave your body and explore the astral realm with confidence and safety.

Achieving your first astral travel experience is always the most difficult—and no single method will work for everyone. That's why the techniques in this book are carefully graded to step by step through an actual out-of-body experience. And with fifteen time-tested methods to choose from you're sure to be astral traveling in no time.

Once you learn to leave your body, the freedom you'll discover will transform your life. Explore new worlds, learn to travel with a partner, go back and forth through time, even find a lover—but, most importantly, lose your fear of death as you discover that you are a spiritual being independent of your physical body.

1-56718-796-X
256 pp., 5³⁄₁₆ x 8 $13.95

I CHING FOR BEGINNERS

A Modern Interpretation of the Ancient Oracle

Mark McElroy

For more than three thousand years, the I Ching has offered guidance to emperors, generals, and philosophers. Amazingly accurate, this ancient oracle anticipates change and recommends timely action in all the important areas of your life.

With clear summaries of each of the I Ching's sixty-four passages, this friendly divination book makes it fun and easy to consult the beloved classic—and all you need is pocket change or a deck of cards. Call upon the wisdom of the I Ching to guide you through life's challenges and rewards!

0-7387-0744-9

312 pp., 5³⁄₁₆ x 8 $14.95